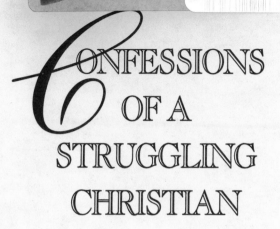

CONFESSIONS OF A STRUGGLING CHRISTIAN

CONFESSIONS OF A STRUGGLING CHRISTIAN

*Learning to
be More like Christ in the
Gray Areas of Life.*

JIM TOOMBS

MULTNOMAH BOOKS

CONFESSIONS OF A STRUGGLING CHRISTIAN

published by Multnomah Books
a part of the Questar publishing family

International Standard Book Number 0-88070-559-0

Printed in the United States of America

For information:
QUESTAR PUBLISHERS, INC.
POST OFFICE BOX 1720
SISTERS, OREGON 97759

93 94 95 96 97 98 99 00 01 02 — 10 9 8 7 6 5 4 3 2 1

Dedication

I dedicate this book to my wife, Mary.
It is no struggle to confess my deep and unrelenting
love for her.

Applause and Thanks

I want to thank the body of Christ that has put up with me through all these struggles as a growing Christian.

My children are a constant source of inspiration to me. Tammy receives what I write with a trusting openness. Rachel keeps me on my toes—it's hard to stay ahead of her intellectually. Michael's encouragement is beyond compare. And Geoffrey is an excellent first reader. They each gave up some of their daddy while this book was being written. Thanks, kids.

Max Lucado has been a generous and encouraging guide and friend through it all. Writing a book can be a very frustrating process. On several occasions, had he not been there with his kind words, I doubt I would have cleared the next hurdle. His humility, humor, and use of nouns and verbs are a model to follow.

Carol Bartley has been a warm-hearted and patient editor on my first book. She has a gift for seeing the heart of a matter. Her contributions have gone beyond the grammatical and the stylistic.

My brother, Jesus, has revealed himself in so many powerful ways. Sometimes I am so much in awe of him I can hardly speak. His really is the name above all names and the only name truly worth confessing.

My gratitude goes to the Holy Spirit for his guidance and counsel.

And my thanks to my Abba for never closing the throne room and never changing the locks.

Contents

Contents

Foreword

This book will test your self-control.

I intended to read only one chapter. Just the first. But I liked it so much I decided to read a second. Just one more I told myself. Then I read a third and a fourth. It's hard to stop reading a book this creative and honest.

In *Confessions of a Struggling Christian* Jim Toombs interweaves struggles and Scripture and gives us a tapestry of hope. He pulls back the curtain on his own life and bids us witness his journey in faith. This isn't the biography of a too-good-to-be-you saint. It is, instead, a collage of reflections on tough topics by a good heart. It's an honor to encourage you to read them.

It's also an honor to introduce you to Jim Toombs. Jim and I have been co-workers for more than five years. I have grown to love his soul and respect his skill. This is his first book. I hope it's not his last.

As you read, you'll be surprised at his candor and inspired at his conclusions.

The chapters are tight. The points are vivid. The illustrations hit close to home. You'll be glad you picked it up.

(Bet you can't read just one chapter.)

Max Lucado

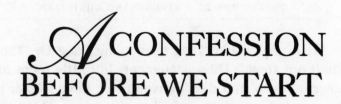

A CONFESSION BEFORE WE START

Life is lived in the vast complexity of the grays.

THOMAS MERTON

CHRISTIANITY IS A CAKEWALK.

At least that's what I thought just four years out of the water of my rebirth. I had examined my life from the high vantage point of my own bellybutton and found myself to be wholly in tune with the Bible. That may have been the single most dangerous time of my life.

I was a black-and-white thinker back then. When I read the Bible, I focused on the dos and the don'ts. Tell me the rules and I would keep them. Or I'd find a way around them. But when the book spoke of "doing God's will," I became frustrated. How was *I* supposed to know God's will? I didn't know my own, let alone his. "His will" was such a loosey-goosey concept for my immature spirit. I wanted rules, not concepts.

"Thou shalt not kill" was more to my liking. Or "Thou shalt not steal." Those statements left little room for interpretation. You didn't have to be a Bible scholar to know what was right and what was wrong. Don't kill anybody. Don't take something that doesn't belong to you. They were simple, straightforward rules, powerful and rigid, though they carried an ominous threat of punishment. But their rigidity cut both ways. Because I was unlikely to kill anyone or steal anything, I stood justified before I ever got out of the chute. I liked that.

One day, in the Sermon on the Mount, I found something that mildly surprised me. Jesus said calling your brother "Raca" was as serious as murder. That was a harsh teaching but not one I thought I really had to worry about—I had never called anyone "Raca" and wasn't likely to. The word wasn't even in my vocabulary. I was further relieved when I learned that "raca" meant "fool." I had never called anyone a "fool." "Stupid." "Idiot." "Dumbo brains," maybe. But not "fool." Mom told us never to call anyone a fool. So again I felt vindicated. And again I missed the boat.

Awhile later I read a really hard teaching. Jesus is separating the sheep and the goats on the last day.[1] He decides who was good and who was bad by how we treated him. But not him. It was how we treated "the least of these," because in them we were to see the Savior.

"You mean, Jesus, that you expect me to see you in the rude clerk at the convenience store? You want me to see you in the dirty, smelly wino who's belching a request for spare change in my face? You expect me to see the Son of God in people who are retarded, and poor, and powerful, and abusive, and mean, as well as in those who are kind, and gentle, and holy? That's a tall order, Jesus."

But it's what he wants.

These "little" encounters at convenience stores and on street corners and at water coolers are the moments that make up our lives. The big times—when we are asked to give up our lives for Jesus or write a big check to help pay for a new roof for the church building or to house a family whose home has been flattened by a tornado—are few. If I wait for those times to practice my Christianity, it will atrophy from lack of use. And I may not know how to use it. I might have forgotten how. Or never really learned.

Becoming like Jesus is not an event; it's a process. It is similar to the Arabic "death from a thousand cuts," only it is life from a thousand choices. Each event builds on the ones preceding it to make me more and more like my Master. To paraphrase a Chinese proverb, "The spiritual journey of a thousand miles begins with one single step."

And so the central question becomes "How will I get to be like Jesus, behaving as he would have me behave in the big situations, if I don't behave like Jesus in the everyday, mundane situations?"

That question has been a spur both for my spiritual struggles over the last several years and for the writing of these "confessions." Yet writing a book like this is risky. I am not a paragon of the Christian walk. Far from it. At times I have taken missteps on my journey to develop the character of Christ. You will read about some of those failures. But even when I have failed to live up to what he wants me to be, I have won. Because always I have grown.

That's the nature of walking with Jesus. What Satan intends for evil, God turns to good.[2]

Reading a book like this can be risky, too. It might change you. It might make the spiritual houseshoes you've grown to love bind a bit. You may find yourself looking at life and the people around you differently when you finish. You may find that you are uncomfortable with life as usual.

Our lives—yours and mine—are the battleground on which the broad struggle between light and darkness is being fought. Jesus came into the world to ensure Satan's defeat. And when he had done so, God seated him at his right hand, and all of creation, both in heaven and on earth, was put under his authority.[3] One of our jobs is to free the captives and to hold our ground against that day when Jesus will return. Until then, the Adversary will continue to accuse us to one another—and to ourselves. He will attempt to foment rebellion on earth as he did in heaven. He will tell lies and plot murders. Yet his efforts are futile, because Jesus has already won the war and paraded the enemy in disgrace before the people.[4]

While we are holding our ground, while we are becoming like Jesus, we need help. So Jesus sent his Holy Spirit to use our bodies as his home. He counsels us and comforts us in hard times. When we have our convenience store encounters, when we gather around the water cooler, he is there, giving us his wisdom in that still, small voice God loves to use. And his light is always shining out of Christians as an unrelenting harassment of the Evil One and as never-ending comfort to those of us struggling along the way.

Christianity is no cakewalk, but it is a glorious walk. Every step is momentous. None is small.

My prayer is that this book will help you recognize and appreciate each of those steps and make more and more of your daily choices—those decisions that hang in the gray between absolute right and absolute wrong—for his glory.

Jim Toombs
San Antonio
June 1993

IN THE BEGINNING...

In the beginning was the Word,
and the Word was with God,
and the Word was God.

JOHN 1:1

I AM. The great, cosmic, ever-present reality.

He thinks, and time is born. He broods, and the universe explodes into being. His essence hovers over a formless ball of gases, and a world is created, teeming with life. Of all, one life form is unique. Humanity alone carries the likeness of the Creator himself.

I AM beholds his handiwork, and his voice rings out, "It is good."

Yet, the creation is not without its problems. Like I AM, humanity has a self. And with it, a self-will. As light cannot be appreciated apart from darkness, and freedom means nothing if there is no prospect of slavery, obedience is empty without the possibility of disobedience. Increasingly this self-willed creature called Man chooses disobedience.

I AM's countenance darkens. His heart is heavy. He regrets having ever made these creatures. They choose with such flippancy to cut themselves off from the source of life. They hear and see, and yet they do not understand.

But he has compassion for the people. A plan is formed, and the Son chooses to become one of them. He will walk in their shoes. He will understand them. And he will save them.

So, on a starry, starry night, in a small cave, in a tiny village, in a remote little country, the Son becomes a baby.

His birth is no less harsh than the countless ones that have gone before. He is rudely ejected from his place of warmth and binding comfort within the womb of the young teenager, into the harsh, cold, unbounded world. His cry echoes off the rock walls, off the inquisitive faces of the sheep and the donkey, off the smiling face of the man who will be known as his father. The Son has become a baby.

He is a good baby (as if a baby could be anything but good). He cries only when his few needs go unmet. When he is wet or soiled, he wails until he is dry and warm. When the emptiness in his stomach becomes a body-sized ache, he trumpets his royal displeasure. His mother bares her full breast and guides his frantic mouth to its target. He suckles, and a sigh of satisfaction escapes through his nose as peace overtakes him once again.

The baby grows as all human babies do...slowly. And the Son discovers what it means to be finite. He is bound by time and the frailty of his body. It lacks coordination. And the mind that spoke his own mother into existence struggles with the concepts of simple arithmetic and the complexities of language. He learns the difficulty, and the satisfaction, of sawing a straight line, of making a smooth joint between two pieces of wood. His hormones surge and his body changes. His voice deepens; his beard grows. And he feels the stirrings of adolescence. The Son has become a young man.

The young man's father grows old and dies. The face of the God/man crumples with pain as the young man folds the rough hands which held his on so many journeys to the great city. His fingers touch those quiet lips which taught him the holy verses. He watches as the women wrap the lifeless body and anoint it with aloes and myrrh as it lies in the simple crypt. His tears fall freely, and his chest aches as every human chest aches. The Son has become a man.

One day the Evil One comes like a moonless night to darken the soul of the man. He is in the desert of both his country and of his soul. For forty days and nights he has fasted. He is weak. He is hungry. He thirsts.

"Turn these rocks into bread," says the Prince of Darkness. "Call on your father's messengers to protect you. Stop kidding yourself. You're not God's son. He doesn't even know you're alive. He has abandoned you as he always abandons his children in times of need. In the most private part of your heart, didn't you always fear it would be so? Pray to me and I will make sure you never suffer another night like the one you just spent!"

Anger flashes in the Son's eyes. His bent and weary frame snaps to as he recalls the words of both his fathers. "Get away from me, you tale-bearer! Man needs more than bread to survive. It is God's word that brings life. And no one deserves prayers but God alone!" The words come in a pant, more forceful in the man's head than in his mouth. For he is weak. And the words of the Evil One have tempted him, for in them lies a hint of truth. Yet he bears the test, and the Evil One flees until a more opportune time. Heaven rejoices at the strength of the Son. And, smiling at this victory, I AM sends his servants to attend him. They nurse his body, and his soul, and his spirit.

The man becomes an itinerant accompanied by a band of devoted followers. Many nights he sleeps on hard ground, his rest interrupted by crawling ants or stubborn pebbles. His feet are cold. Mosquitoes buzz in his ears and suck the blood from his body. Sometimes there are beds in strange houses or pallets of straw. Always he talks about I AM. Whatever he does, and he does much, focuses attention on I AM.

And when the strangeness becomes too strange or the people want too much, when the temptations threaten to return, the Son retires to a distance and spends the night in quiet conversation with the Father.

Wherever he goes he is loved. He performs feats no man has ever performed. He heals the sick. He makes the lame walk. At his touch, the blind see. Yet not all the blind are able to see. For theirs is a blindness not of the eye but of the soul. Darkness is their constant companion, and they do not understand the light of the Son. To them, blinded by the Prince of Darkness, he is incomprehensible. In their confusion they lash out in anger and fear. They lash out at the Son who has become a man.

He is betrayed. He is abandoned. The Evil One says, "I told you so!" The Son is beaten. He is nailed to a cross and killed. But as he dies, the expected curses never come from his lips. For as he dies, he dies with compassion for even the blind of heart who have taken his life. As he refused in the desert to yield to temptation, so he refuses to prove his divinity by saving himself at the cross. Once again the Evil One draws no blood. Once again he flees. Yet this time he bolts in fear. This time he flees in panic. For this time the man has become the Savior.

Yet for a while the Son remains. For forty days he encourages his followers. He holds their hands as if they were little children and he their father. They are comforted. After a while they realize their loss was no loss at all. The love of the Son who became a man has strengthened them beyond fear, beyond failure.

Though battles remain, victory has been won. The Son returns to I AM, leaving his Spirit to comfort and guide those who follow him in the struggle that remains.

COLDER THAN THE NIGHT

His wife said to him, "Are you still holding on to your integrity?
Curse God and die!"

He replied, "You are talking like a foolish woman.
Shall we accept good from God, and not trouble?"

In all this, Job did not sin in what he said.

JOB 2:9-10

THE NIGHT IS BITTER and still. It is February 1974, and
even in San Antonio it is cold. The sky is clear as crystal,
and the stars hang from invisible threads in the moonless
ebony of the heavens. Orion the hunter commands the
southeastern sky, lying on his back, his sword ready to slay
great bears and small ones, scorpions and goats. His
faithful dog sits at his feet.

"I don't love you like I used to," she had told me the
week before.

I looked into her eyes, listening to the cracking of my
heart. I saw a shadow flicker across her face. "Is there
someone else?" I asked.

She paused, her eyes downcast. "Yes. But you'll find
someone else. Lots of women would love to have you."

Lots of women. Just not my wife. Not the woman who bore my children. Not the woman who helped me find Christ. Not the woman I swore to love for the rest of my life nor the woman who swore to love me.

Our home is on the edge of town. Out back, a dirt road meanders along the rim of a cliff, overlooking a wild creek bed. In happier times it was one of my favorite places, green and feral. Tonight it is as desolate and austere as my soul.

A tremendous weight bears down on my breastbone, crushing my heart. Suddenly I want to run. My legs begin pumping on their own. I sprint in the blackness barely able to tell the dual gray ribbons of the roadbed from the black field. As I run, my breaths come deeper and faster. I run and I run. The pain keeps pace with me, my ever present companion. My feet hammer the ground and the sound is lost in the night. Now my lungs are on fire. "Nooooo!" I scream. Suddenly my legs stop. I lean over, gasping for breath, wishing for tears that will not come.

Where is God? How long must I cry for help before he listens?[1] My fists clench as I raise my eyes toward heaven.

"Where are you? Can't you hear me? Why don't you do something? Do my prayers mean nothing to you? Why don't you stop this?"

My words are swallowed by the night as they leave my lips. I feel empty and dreadfully alone.

Is this the way Job felt when he was tempted to curse the Almighty? Did Jesus feel this way in the wilderness? Perhaps, but they were spiritual giants. Not me.

It has been only four years since I became a follower of Christ. Four years to build my faith from a mustard seed to a coriander seed. My progress has been slow. But through a weekly study with friends I have become convicted of the saving grace of God, manifested in both the Old and the New Testaments.

Yet I have felt a distance between myself and sin-besieged humanity. I have no problems. Everything in my life is just great. Nothing challenges my faith.

Until now. Now an overwhelming weight presses against the miniscule seed of my faith. Will it be crushed to dust, scattered by the north wind? Or can it withstand the test?

Suddenly I feel an affinity for Job I have never felt before. I can see down the road to the loss of my marriage. My children will be ripped from me, and I will be relegated to part-time parent. Weekend daddy. We have not been financially strong, but now I will be devastated. I will lose my home and move into an apartment. I will never see the fruit from the little orchard we planted. I will pay child support from my small paycheck.

Part of me rails at the injustice. And a smaller part asks honestly, *What was your part in all this? It takes two to make a marriage, doesn't it?* Yeah, but it takes only one to mess it up. *Not true—you know there are always three sides to every marriage problem: her side, his side, and the truth.* Yeah, but she's not trying. It's her fault, I pout to myself. And the wounded part wins, for now.

In my mind's eye I see the caliche road on which I stand forking into two branches. The one on the right leads to the God who has failed me. The one on the left into the pit.

"How could you do this to me?" I scream. The tears are finally forming in my eyes. "How could you abandon me like this? Why don't you answer me? Why are you so far away?"

Why am *I* so far away? Is it me? God alone knows my own culpability in this whole mess. I can't see it yet, though deep in my heart I know it is there. To reject God now wouldn't be right. It would be unfair, blaming him for my own shortcomings. But my human nature urges me to find a scapegoat rather than inflict any more pain on myself.

Anger burns my face as I look at the fork. I feel like a petulant child. This is it, I think. This is my crossroads. I can choose to stand with God, or I can choose to walk away from him. That will show him. He doesn't deserve my loyalty. Yet...yet, there has been so much I have not understood, so many times I have missed the point. Perhaps I don't understand now what is happening. Perhaps this is the time when faith must stand strong, even when the wind is blowing so hard my faith can hardly stand at all.

I look to the imaginary fork. On the left lies blackness and oblivion. A great void. It is colder there. And lonely. Then my gaze shifts to the right. This road is also shrouded in darkness, but the lights of the distant city and the other houses bring light to the gloom. It is warmer and more vital than the road to the pit.

Looking to Heaven, to God, my Abba, I say, "You've got me, don't you, Daddy? I can't turn away from you. There really is no place to go. I have to trust you. I have no other choice."

I long to feel his hands on my shoulders, his arms around me. I want to feel myself pressed to his strong, warm chest. But I don't. In the numbness of my pain I don't feel much of anything.

The rocks crunch beneath my feet as I turn towards my home. I have faced the most critical choice of my young spiritual life. And I have chosen the way home.

I begin walking and the wind sighs.

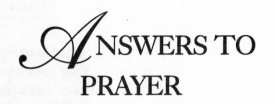ANSWERS TO PRAYER

He went to the house of Mary the mother of John, also called Mark, where many people had gathered and were praying. Peter knocked at the outer entrance, and a servant girl named Rhoda came to answer the door. When she recognized Peter's voice, she was so overjoyed she ran back without opening it and exclaimed, "Peter is at the door!"

"You're out of your mind," they told her. When she kept insisting that it was so, they said, "It must be his angel."

ACTS 12:12-15

MOVING TO ABILENE, Texas, was an answer to prayer.

I know that may be hard to believe, especially if you've ever been there.

Abilene is in a flat, semiarid region almost devoid of trees and ground water. You can draw a circle with a two-hundred-mile radius and not hit any town of any size. Wasteland is a kind word to describe the area, (though native West Texans and Chamber of Commerce folks will take issue with that statement). It is far different from the lake-loaded hills around Austin where I grew up. But it was a new start for me and a definite answer to prayer.

After my divorce I languished in San Antonio for a year, continuing to write and produce advertising at a local advertising agency. But I was getting nowhere financially. Well, that's not exactly true. I was getting somewhere, but I was going in the opposite direction from that which I had always intended. Each month I was just barely able to keep afloat in an ever-deepening pool of red ink.

The advertising business on the local scene was never going to be lucrative. I had pretty much topped out in my earnings. Yet the divorce had left me with more bills and less money. I felt the urgent need to change careers.

I also needed a change of scenery. Much of what I saw every day reminded me of my wife and children and the life we would never have together. I longed for a new place, a new start.

I had also been praying for God to send me some spiritually strong, male friends. Becoming suddenly single had shown me how difficult it was to fit into the church as a solo act. My friends had been mostly *our* friends. Now there was no longer a "we," only an "I." I felt that though my presence was tolerated I made my friends uncomfortable when I was around. Or maybe I was the one who was uncomfortable. Either way I needed some friends—male friends who knew Jesus better than I did.

I prayed for these things every day, morning and night. My prayers were at least a fleece; at worst they were arrogance. I had read the promise: "Ask and it will be given to you....For everyone who asks receives....If you...know how to give good gifts to your children, how much more will your Father in heaven give good gifts to those who ask him!"[1]

I was calling God's hand. I desperately wanted the promise to be true. If my prayer was arrogant, it was also a prayer of anguish. And one of desperate faith. I had no alternative. God was my only hope.

I learned at least two things about God from this whole situation. First, he answers prayer. Those aren't just empty whisperings we send out into the air. He hears and he answers. Second, he is efficient. If I come to him with a whole passel of needs, why should he provide for them with a whole passel of answers when one will do?

That's what happened. In one grand act God gave me a new place to live, a 30 percent increase in my salary, and an exciting new career. Hey, three out of four ain't bad.

But he was saving the best for later.

Finding an apartment was really tough in Abilene. It is a college town of about one hundred thousand with three church schools—Baptist, Methodist, and Church of Christ—and an air force base. Demand for apartments far exceeded supply.

After days of looking I was fortunate to find a nice apartment on the northeast side of town. It was perfect because it was just three minutes from the office. What a change from San Antonio where I fought freeway gridlock for forty-five minutes every day!

It was also perfect in that it had two bedrooms. That meant when I made the nine-hour round trip each month to get my two daughters I would have a nice place for them to stay, with their own room. God had answered my prayers beyond my expectations.

About three months after I moved in I realized that a 30 percent increase in my salary was not as much as I thought it would be. The extra room in the apartment put an extra strain on my cash flow, as did the monthly trips to get the girls. And I didn't have those male friends yet, either.

So I went back to the prayer well: Lord, I feel a little foolish asking for more money, but you can see things aren't working out like I had planned. And I still haven't met those friends you were going to connect me with. Would you please help me?

It was a simple prayer. But, again, one I prayed two or three times a day. I took Paul as literally as I could. I tried to pray without ceasing. Except when I was watching my favorite TV program.

That was "Happy Days" on Tuesday night. I didn't watch much television, but I thought Fonzie and the Cunningham family were worth my time. They were funny, light, and wholesome.

It's interesting that the two men chose Tuesday night to come by. I was sitting on my sofa watching TV when a knock came at my door. I was immediately irritated by the interruption.

As I opened the door, there stood Herb Butrum. Herb worked in fund-raising for Abilene Christian. I had met him at church, and we had talked a bit. He had asked me just a week ago if I was interested in a roommate. I had told him emphatically, "No!" Apparently not emphatically enough.

The young man with him was tall. And red-headed. And red-bearded. He wore a plaid shirt and blue jeans. He looked like a lumberjack outfitted by GQ.

"Hi, Jim. This is Mike Blanton," Herb said as he ushered the redhead into my home.

I didn't like this at all. I'd never seen this Blanton guy before, and I hardly knew Herb. I didn't like them intruding on my favorite TV show.

"He's the fellow I told you about. Mike just moved here from Nashville to work for the Chamber of Commerce."

I realized we were all standing in the living room with our hands hanging out. I grinned inside at their discomfort and let it linger just a moment before I offered them a chair.

"Have a seat," I said. "I was just watching my favorite TV program." I continued to let the set blare. Boy, was I being a jerk.

"Mike's been having a hard time finding an apartment," shouted Herb.

"It's a tight market," I conceded at the top of my voice. "Have you tried Le Dumpola? The manager told me they might have something about this time."

The redhead yelled. "I called but they're full."

"Have you tried the want ads?"

"We've tried everything. There just isn't any place available," said Herb, turning down the TV.

I could believe that. If it hadn't been for the grace of God, I would not have found my cozy two-bedroom.

Herb continued, "That's why I wanted you to meet Mike. I thought at the very worst you might be able to let him move in for a month or two until he finds another apartment."

Oh, sure. A month or two. I used to have a dog like that. "Oh, please let me just put my nose on your leg. That's all, just my nose." It wasn't long before the rest of him followed. First the nose, then both forelegs wrapped around my head, and then a big, hairy body deposited itself in my lap. I looked at Mike's nose. I was beginning to feel cornered.

"I...I don't think so. Nope. You see, I got this big apartment so my daughters would have a room of their own when they visited. Did I tell you I was divorced?" I added the last sentence like Professor Van Helsing showing Count Dracula his new cross. What Christian in his right mind would want to share a room with someone with a fresh *D* branded on his forehead? I found out.

"That's okay. I'll take the smaller bedroom if you like." The redhead again.

Of course he'd take the smaller bedroom. I wasn't giving up my nice big master bedroom to anybody. Wait a minute. What was I saying? This guy wasn't going to live here!

I began shaking my head as I got off the couch and paced across the room. "Listen, this just isn't going to work out. I've only had one roommate, and she didn't work out. I've got two beautiful daughters who don't need to be growing up around a bunch of strange men. And I don't know how we'd work out the kitchen stuff. I can see it now. I'll buy food and you'll eat it; you'll leave dirty dishes all over, and I'll have to clean them up. And what if I want to have a girl over? How do we work out things like that? Huh? Huh?"

Mike looked over at me with his smiling blue eyes and gently said, "Well, brother, I don't see how we can have any problems if we both love the Lord."

First I pulled my body off the kitchen wall. That was hard because the sword had gone all the way through me. Then I pulled it out of my heart and said, "Come on. Let me show you your room."

It was typical me. I spent all that time praying for close, spiritually mature male friends and some way to free up my cash flow, and then I worked just as hard to resist the working of God's spirit.

But God is stronger than I am. And he is more faithful. His faithfulness teaches me how to be faithful.

My friendship with Mike blossomed, and he became an important part of my life for a few years. Now he is back in Nashville, the successful producer of some of the more prominent names in Christian music today. Time and distance have weakened the worldly ties between us, but nothing will ever erode the bond we share in Jesus Christ.

Is there a moral to this story? I think so. When you pray to God, get out of the way. Let him work. Accept the answer he gives you. Don't quench his Holy Spirit. And be careful to whom you open your door; you may be entertaining red-headed angels unawares.

ℒOOKING FOR THE LOOPHOLE

If any of you has a dispute with another, dare he take it before the ungodly for judgment instead of before the saints? Do you not know that we will judge angels? How much more the things of this life! Therefore, if you have disputes about such matters, appoint as judges even men of little account in the church!...Why not rather be wronged? Why not rather be cheated?

1 CORINTHIANS 6:1, 3-4, 7

I WALKED INTO THE attorney's office, introduced myself, and promptly lay on the floor. Although she was a member of the large church my family and I had been attending, we had never met.

"Are you all right?" she asked, alarm and concern tightening her face as she surveyed the sling around my fractured collarbone.

"I'm okay," I said. "I just need to lie down to keep the room from spinning."

"He got sick on the way over here, and we had to pull over for a few minutes," explained Mary, my wife of less than a year.

"I'll be fine. I know it's a little weird, but can we do this with me lying on the floor?"

"Well, I guess so. I mean, it won't bother me." The attorney had regained most of her composure. "It's good to finally meet you, Mr. Toombs. I have had an opportunity to review all the documents you sent me, and it is my opinion that you have an excellent case. The defendant can be prosecuted under the Sherman Antitrust laws. That's good news for us because there is statutorily mandated restitution of treble damages for injured parties."

"Whoa," I said. "Could we try that last part again? In English?"

"What I'm saying is that you won't have to bring a civil suit to get compensated for being run out of business. Nor will there be any need to prove anything beyond actual damages, which I estimate to be between $50,000 and $80,000. Since they violated the Sherman Antitrust laws, they have to pay you three times your actual damages. That means you stand to gain between $150,000 and $250,000."

"Wow! That ought to get their attention. What do you think our chances are?" I asked.

"Excellent! It's as close to a laydown, pat hand as I've seen. What you have given me is essentially a smoking gun. If we can get a judge to hear the case, as opposed to a jury, our chances will be even better."

"So, now I just have to decide whether to sue or not. If I don't, I stand to lose a lot of money. And I'll have to get outta Dodge. On the other hand, if I do sue, we can make a small fortune. And we end up dragging Jesus' name through the court system."

"What do you mean?"

"I mean these guys are Christians. Even though they don't act like it."

"So? They have ruined your business and they're bullying you. Christians or not, they've bought some pretty big trouble."

That was all true enough.

I had gone into competition with my former employers, probably not the smartest move of my life. Their response had been vicious and brutal. And it hadn't stopped with my business. They wanted to destroy me, and they would destroy my family to do it. Mary, a nurse, had been working in the intensive care unit at one of the local hospitals. One of my former employers had a lot of pull in that hospital, and he had used his sizeable influence to make things very uncomfortable for her. Her supervisor as much as told her so. Just so he could get back at me.

Then there were the other three prongs of their attack. We were all believers worshiping at the same congregation. My three adversaries had brought our conflict before the elders for their help in resolving it. It didn't help my case that one of the three was himself an elder. And it hurt that they were simultaneously trying to shut me down through threats of lawsuit and other legal maneuvers at the same time they were trying to have the church leaders resolve the issue.

One of them, a man with whom I had worked closely for two years, also paid a visit to a potential employer of mine in a large city two hundred miles away. He actually sat in the man's house and told lie after lie about my abilities and my integrity in an attempt to block any chance of my being hired.

No, I wouldn't soon lose sight of what these people had done to me and my family. Forgiving would be difficult, forgetting all but impossible.

I was having a very difficult time holding on to Jesus' commands to love your enemy, to turn the other cheek, and to give my coat to the guy who was suing me for my shirt.[1] I never expected to have to apply those hard teachings about loving my enemy. I never thought I would have a real enemy. Now here I was, eight years after putting on Jesus as Lord, up to my chin in temptation and opportunity. Not to mention anger.

That's why Mary thinks God broke my collarbone. Someone had said, "Let's play touch football after church. We'll let the girls play, too." That last phrase was what hooked me. I had sworn off football after fracturing my elbow the year before. I was getting too old to be slamming my body into other guys' bodies on a Sunday afternoon. But if the girls play, everybody will take it easy, right?

Wrong. It was a typical sandlot game: everybody's eligible. So when the quarterback hefted the ball into the air, I raced toward it. I never saw the other guy. Somebody said he was on my team, though I had never seen him before. I don't know where he came from, but we collided just as the ball was floating down into my arms. I heard the bone snap and crunch as we smacked into one another.

Mary took me to the emergency room where they put a figure-eight clavicle strap on. The pain was terrible at first. After it subsided, the vertigo and nausea began. It was hard to make it through the day let alone run a business and fight legal and spiritual battles. That's why Mary thinks God did it. I don't know about the theology of that, but I know the starch had gone out of my sails. And I was much more compliant than I might have otherwise been.

"Doesn't the Bible say it's better to be cheated by your brother than to take him to court?" I asked the attorney.[2]

She answered slowly. "Are you referring to when Paul was addressing the Corinthian church's penchant for lawsuits?"

"Yes, I am. How do you deal with that as a Christian attorney?"

"It's not easy. Frankly, I believe Paul was talking about Christians who were using the courts much as they are being used today—for undue enrichment and for settling petty squabbles. But I don't think that's what is going on here. You have been truly wronged, in a big way. The only way you will get redress is in a court of law. Besides, I'm not even sure these people are your brothers. They certainly aren't acting like it. They seem to be wrapping themselves in the church when it's convenient, and taking it off when it's not. Christianity is like your skin, not like a piece of clothing you take on and off to suit yourself or other people."

I was beginning to be real uncomfortable talking about lawsuits. "Hmmm. I guess that knife cuts both ways, doesn't it? I mean isn't this a 'sauce for the goose is sauce for the gander' kind of argument? Here I am condemning them for taking me to court, and I'm talking about suing them."

"Mr. Toombs, I understand what you are saying. You may do as you wish and, of course, however you feel God is leading you. But it is both my legal and biblical opinion that you have every right to sue these people and seek redress before the law."

Although I heard her words, I wasn't sure I agreed. This was not going to be an easy decision.

When he was on the mountain overlooking the Sea of Galilee, Jesus told the people many hard things. Perhaps the hardest was to forsake revenge and to love your enemies.

The natural human response is to say, "Yeah, but he didn't mean in this situation." I call it looking for the loophole. The only problem is that Jesus didn't leave any loopholes.

Jesus said,

You have heard that it was said, "Eye for eye, and tooth for tooth." But I tell you, Do not resist an evil person. If someone strikes you on the right cheek, turn to him the other also. And if someone wants to sue you and take your tunic, let him have your cloak as well. If someone forces you to go one mile, go with him two miles. Give to the one who asks you, and do not turn away from the one who wants to borrow from you.

Love your enemies and pray for those who persecute you, that you may be sons of your Father in heaven....Be perfect, therefore, as your heavenly Father is perfect.[3]

Do you see any loopholes there? I don't. Jesus is telling me, "The old law said you could seek revenge against your brother, but I'm changing all that." The old law called for the punishment to fit the crime. If someone poked your eye out, you could poke his out. If someone killed your servant, you could kill his servant. If a person stole your car, you could take his car. That is fundamental, tit-for-tat justice.

But people—like me—don't want justice. We want revenge. You take a pound of my flesh, and I'll take two pounds of yours. You shoot my dog, and I'll shoot your cow. You steal my car, and I'll blow up your whole house. If you poke my eye out, I want to do more than just poke your eye out. I want to poke out both your eyes, burn your barn, and take your wife. Why? Because my flesh, my dog, my car, and my eye, since they belong to *me*, are more valuable than anything of *yours*. That's because I am more valuable than you are...at least from my perspective. So I have to hurt you more than you hurt me. The trading of eyes is justice. The escalation of retribution is revenge. And there is no end to it. That is how feuds start and continue. And that is how wars start. Is it any wonder that God, in his wisdom, said that vengeance belonged to him, not to us?

Jesus doesn't even want us to get justice. He wants us to turn the other cheek and all that stuff. Now, where's the loophole in that? No wonder the Jews got mad at him! An eye for an eye makes more sense to our human nature than to love our enemy. At least it allows some sense of revenge. And, besides, it certainly seems more in keeping with the old covenant.

That's basically the argument I had with myself as I struggled through the problem of suing my brothers. But it was a flawed argument.

The Old Testament has a lot more to say about vengeance and justice than "eye for eye."

> Do not seek revenge or bear a grudge against one of your people, but love your neighbor as yourself. I am the Lord.[4]

> He who mocks the poor shows contempt for their Maker; whoever gloats over disaster will not go unpunished.[5]

> Do not say, "I'll do to him as he has done to me; I'll pay that man back for what he did."[6]

> If your enemy is hungry, give him food to eat; if he is thirsty, give him water to drink.[7]

Revenge is what my enemies were doing to me. And, it is what I wanted to do to them. I wanted to hurt them back for hurting my wife. I wanted to cut back for their damaging my reputation, hurting my business, and harming my opportunity for employment.

And, I wanted to get rich. Yeah, the money was quite a draw. Two hundred and fifty thousand dollars is a quarter of a million dollars. People retire on less money. My folks sure did. Most people never even get close to that kind of cash.

And I wanted to win. I was taught how to lose gracefully, but I was never good at it. Winning was a lot easier. And a whole lot more fun. I didn't want to lose to these guys. It would hurt my pride.

Perhaps that was the biggest stumbling block of all: my pride. Pride was behind the desire for revenge. Stick their thumb in my eye, will they. Don't they know who I am? And pride was definitely behind my desire to win. Nobody remembers a loser. Nobody writes books about them. And nobody invites them to be on corporate boards or to sing the national anthem at an NBA game.

After Mary and I had prayed almost continually for a week, I called the attorney.

"We have decided not to go forward with the lawsuit," I told her.

"For heaven's sake, why not?" she asked.

"Precisely."

ℒIVING FOR THE MOMENT

"The King will reply, 'I tell you the truth, whatever you did for one of the least of these brothers of mine, you did for me.'"

MATTHEW 25:40

I PARK IN THE GLOOM beside the convenience store. As I slam the car door, too late I see him lurching toward me out of the darkness. His steps are unsteady, but his track is sure. I am his target. I am his next victim.

"You're a nice-lookin' young man," he growls in a voice full of gravel and saliva.

I try to ignore him. Yet even as I angle my walk to miss him, I know it is hopeless. I step up onto the sidewalk, and he turns. He raises his arm and points at me. "Now, I'm not going to lie to you. No sir. I'm nuthin' but a drunk. And I need a drink. You got any spare change?"

I look into his face and smell the yeasty, sour vapors of his breath. His beard is three or four days old. And as a constant backdrop to the smell of his breath, comes the acrid odor of cigarettes, long dead. His pants and out-of-style sport coat are gray and rumpled like his life.

What would Jesus have done? Perhaps he would have healed the man with a word. Or maybe he would have said something riveting and penetrating that would have cut through to the man's heart. But I'm not Jesus. This man doesn't want to hear any sermons. He doesn't want to make any meaningful connections with anyone. People have only used him and hurt him. They are not worth the risk. His body may be vulnerable, but his soul is not. He is like a heavily armored, iron-clad sailing ship, battering willy-nilly into people's lives, yet protected from their love or their rejections by the callouses life has wrapped around his soft, vital parts.

Besides, I have come for a gallon of milk, not a moment in eternity. A quarter would keep him at bay and send him ricocheting after his next mark. In spite of myself, compassion begins to warm my heart as I reach into my pocket and pull out my money clip.

"How about a buck?" I say as I peel off the old, wrinkled bill.

His eyes follow every move. They are riveted on the few bills in my hand. He pauses and I think, Dummy! What are you doing, showing this guy where your money is! Now he's trying to decide whether to knock you in the head and rob you or just breathe on you some more!

The man holds out his grimy hand for me to shake. Surprised and speechless, I stick my hand out, too. As I do, he surprises me again by saying, "May God bless you ever day of your life!

"I'm sixty-four years old. I'm a wino. I been through

World War II, Korea, and Vietnam, and you're the first guy's ever given me a dollar bill." Whether his eyes are misty from rheuminess or emotion I'm not sure. But suddenly his walls are gone. I see the real man, in all his vulnerability and pain.

Looking into those eyes, I say, "That's what I want for you, too. I want God to bless you."

"You know I'm going to buy something to drink with this, don't you?" he asks matter-of-factly. There is a note of honest incredulity in his voice, edged with defiant arrogance.

"Yes, I do."

Our eyes hold one another for a long moment. For a moment we see into each other's souls. For a moment we see the similarities between two men created in God's image. For a moment we see the possibilities. That's what the dollar buys us. A moment.

For a moment I can see through his armor of rumpledness and bad breath, the hair in wild disarray. For a moment I can see Jesus in him. For a moment my eyes behold him as a child of God, a human being created by the same hand that created me.

And then the moment is gone. The steel shutters behind his eyes slam back into their usual place. My own revulsion and fear return. My own attitude of judgment tries to resurrect itself. With a dedicated will I fight it back.

Then the man drops his head and almost scuffs his toe on the ground as he resumes the act that has become his life, "'Course what I really need is a bottle of wine. And you can't get much for a dollar...."

THE GOD OF THE CARBURETOR

"'Love the Lord your God with all your heart and with all your
soul and with all your mind and with all your strength.' The
second is this: 'Love your neighbor as yourself.'
There is no
commandment greater than these."
MARK 12:30-31

IN AUGUST IN SAN ANTONIO it's never cool, not even in the early evening. The humidity's high, the temperature's high, and there's rarely a breeze. That's why what happened that evening made a little sense.

"Dad! There's a guy up the street who needs some water. Can I get him some?" Michael's face was flushed, and he was excited as only an eleven-year-old with a noble purpose can be.

"What do you mean he needs some water?" I asked, my eyes narrowing slightly. I'm a city dweller on a busy street. I also tend to be a tad cynical and enormously protective when it comes to my children.

"He told us to get some water," volunteered Geoffrey. "His car's stopped and he's thirsty."

Now I was even more suspicious. "Well, get him some water then. I'm glad you asked before you took it to him. That shows good judgment." It was a good blend of responsibility and Christian compassion.

"Here, I'll go with you," I said, crawling out of my favorite chair—the one from the Relax Your Back store that conforms to my body and turns me into a puddle of warm jelly.

Michael and Geoffrey headed up the hill where Mulberry intersects Main Avenue, with Michael carefully toting a large plastic cup full of ice water.

At the intersection the kids ran on ahead, and I began to understand the request for water. The man was standing beside an old, black car, his head under the hood. Even from halfway down the block I could see the smoke rising from the front of his car.

As I arrived, Michael was offering a young Hispanic man the water. Slightly out of his teens, if that, the young man stared at the water, shaking his head, his mouth open in a slight grin.

"He thought you were thirsty," I offered.

"No, man. It's the radiator." Pointing to the radiator overflow reservoir, he said, "I took this off and poured the water in, but it all boiled out. I need some water, bad."

"You sure do. Hang tight. I'll be back in a few minutes."

I hoofed it home and grabbed an empty milk jug out of the hall closet and filled it with pure Edward's Aquifer water.

Four trips later it still didn't look good for the 1979 Buick Regal with the T-tops.

"That's why they stole it, man. Those T-tops. I had some locks on 'em until my brother lost the key."

I poured the final jug of water into the steaming radiator. Suddenly I heard the sizzle of boiling water from somewhere off to my left. Not good news. The radiator was to my right. As I turned toward the sound, I saw water bubbling from a broken hose and skittering on the top of the engine.

"Here's your problem," I said. "This hose is busted."

He couldn't believe it. "Oh, man! What am I gonna do now? I ain't got no money to fix it. I got all the tools I need, but I ain't got no money for no parts."

We just stared at the hose and watched the water sizzle away.

Knitting my brow, I looked closer at the hose. "What if you cut off the bad part?"

"Huh?"

"What if you cut off the broken part of the hose? It looks like you'll still have enough hose to do what you need to do."

"What do you do, man?" he asked, with a weird look on his face.

"A lot of things," I said.

He opened his trunk and pulled out a screwdriver and a very sharp hunting knife. "Come on, man, what do you do?"

"I'm a minister," I said, as I glanced from the knife to the three rings in his right ear. "Why?"

"I thought you was a mechanic or something. I'd have never thought to cut that hose off." He was cutting it as he spoke.

"Well that ought to do it," I said hopefully.

"Yeah. Say a good prayer, man. I really need this thing to start."

He sat in the driver's seat and pulled out a long, thin screwdriver. "Mexican starter," he said with a grin. He must have seen my chin drop at the obvious ethnic slur. "That's what my friends call 'em. Mexican starters. Those guys broke this when they stole it. Just stick it in here on these teeth, pull it forward, and..." The engine gave a couple of sick, half-hearted grunts, coughed, clicked, and fell silent. He tried again, getting only a few metallic clicks for his trouble.

I frowned. "This car is stolen?"

He looked up at me through the long black hair that hung over his eyes. "Not anymore. I got it back."

"Oh. Looks like your battery's dead," I said.

He slumped forward in despair and rested his head on the steering wheel.

I put my hand on his shoulder through the window. "I'll be back in a minute. I've got some jumper cables in my car."

Before long my little '86 Honda Prelude was in the middle of the intersection, almost kissing his bruiser of a

Buick Regal. As we connected the battery cables, I wondered if I would talk to this young man about Jesus. And if I did, what would I say?

He climbed behind the wheel of his car and ground the starter—to no effect. His engine turned sluggishly at best.

"Let it sit for a bit," I said. "We'll let your battery charge some."

I returned to my car and raced the engine, sending a constant stream of electrons into his hungry battery. Again he tried. And again the engine refused to catch. And again. And again. And again.

He came around to my side of my car. "I must have already ruined the engine," he said. He was about to cry. I understood how he felt. I had just paid over two thousand dollars for emergency repairs to my plumbing, my washing machine, and my air conditioner. It hurt, but at least I had it. This poor guy looked as if he didn't have two thousand cents.

"Man, a new engine costs what, eight hundred bucks?" The way he said it, it might as well have been a million.

"I guess. I don't know, really. But I don't think it's your engine. I think my battery is too small. Let me get my other car, and I'll be right back. It's about the last trick I've got."

As I pulled the big Plymouth Voyager into the intersection, I wondered what Jesus would have done. And I wondered again what I would tell this desperate young man about my Lord.

We connected the cables, and he tried again. His engine was more robust sounding, and white vapors floated out of his carburetor. But still the engine refused to start.

"Let her charge a little, like we did before," I suggested. "Does your car have an automatic choke?"

He looked at me again as if he couldn't believe I was asking these questions. "I don't know. Why?"

"Because if it's got an automatic choke, every time you try to start it the choke kicks in and shoves gas to the carburetor. If it doesn't start fast, it gets flooded. But to get rid of the flooding, you just push the accelerator to the floor and hold it there while you're cranking. The car will start."

He looked at me again, and I began to realize how those poor insects must feel when they are impaled on a straight pin and their captor is looking at them with that mixture of incredulity, disgust, and awe. I don't look like I know which end of a car to put the gas in, I guess. I could have been wrong, too, since I was making some of it up as I went along. But the explanation sounded good to me.

He tried again. The engine roared, caught for an instant, and died.

He came over once again and stood beside my car. "Almost," he grinned.

I grinned back.

"I can't believe you know so much about cars, man. You knew to cut the hose. And now I know my car's got an automatic choke. I didn't know any of that stuff."

"It's because I'm old. I had the same kind of problems when I was a kid. I learned."

"Hey, it's not because you're old. You just got experience."

I smiled at his attempt to protect me from the negative label of "old."

"Listen, man, I'm sorry for taking up so much of your time tonight, but I really appreciate your help."

"You're welcome," I said. "You know it's because of Jesus."

"Huh?"

"It's because of Jesus. Somebody once asked him what was the most important thing in the world, and he said there were really two things. Number one is to love God with all your heart, soul, and mind. And the second thing was to love your neighbor as yourself. You know, treat other people the way you want to be treated. And if my car was broken like this, I would want someone to stop and help me, too. That's why I helped you."

"That's what I always try to do. Help people. But I never need no help. This is the first time."

"Well, you just keep helping people. God likes that. Why don't we try it again?"

He crawled back under the wheel, hunkered over the steering column, and got his "Mexican starter" in position. I heard his engine roar to life as billows of dark smoke belched from the tailpipe. It was as if God had wanted this young man to hear something special first. Or perhaps he wanted this middle-aged man to say something special and heartfelt. Or maybe he just wanted to challenge both of us in our comfort zones.

At any rate the God of the carburetor acted in his own sweet time. And two of his children, separated by age, culture, and language, were richer for it.

GOOD OLD EBENEZER

"Do not store up for yourselves treasures on earth, where moth and rust destroy, and where thieves break in and steal. But store up for yourselves treasures in heaven, where moth and rust do not destroy, and where thieves do not break in and steal. For where your treasure is, there your heart will be also."

MATTHEW 6:19-21

WHY DO PEOPLE WORK?

It was a serious question.

Especially when making humongous sums of money was so easy!

The year was 1979, and Mary and I had sold our home in the spring. I had made a nice profit of about $10,000 and had been trying to decide the best way to invest such a large sum. It really was a lot of money— more than either of us had ever had in one lump.

I had been reading in the *Wall Street Journal* that silver was beginning to move. It looked like a better investment than real estate, so I called one of the advertisers in the back of the paper who specialized in precious metals.

I learned that with my $10,000 I could control almost $100,000 worth of silver futures contracts. And then, because I was so highly leveraged, for every $.10 the price of silver climbed, I would be making a profit of almost $1700. The guy on the phone told me it was a great time to buy. Silver was at $6.60 an ounce, and "you won't ever see $6.00 silver again!" The Hunt boys were buying every ounce they could get their hands on, driving the price up and up.

So I took the plunge. I invested the whole bankroll in silver futures, without having a real clue as to what I was doing.

The Hunts continued to buy silver—hundreds of millions of ounces of it. And the price of the metal soared. I pyramided my investment, using my paper profits to buy more and more contracts. And silver climbed the charts. On its back rode the other metals: copper, gold, and platinum. I bought them all.

By September, my original $10,000 investment had grown to over $100,000 in profit. I controlled close to a million dollars in precious metals. And still the prices and the profits continued to rise.

I couldn't believe no one had ever told me about this before! It was so easy to make money this way. Lots easier than working. Which raised some important questions. Why did anybody work? Why was I working? Why didn't I just retire? I would pray about that. Retiring. I hadn't really prayed about the investment, but I had asked God to bless it after I made it. And, boy, if he hadn't gone and blessed it to high heaven!

And he continued blessing it.

By November, my profit had doubled to around $200,000. Daily I kept track of the movement of the markets. I spent hours just contemplating my new wealth and what it could mean to my family and me. I ran computer projections, "what-if" scenarios, of silver at various price levels. Then, of course, I had to calculate what would happen to my other metals holdings if silver were to go up so much. The bottom line was always bigger and bigger.

It was an incredible time. I was often lost in daydreams about where we would go, what we would do. Think of the places we could travel. Rome, Paris, London. We could move to a larger home, buy a nice car—with air conditioning. And if silver were to rise another $10 or $20 an ounce, and if I continued to invest so wisely, no telling what God would allow.

It was great being his anointed one.

But there was a problem. My job. I found it hard to enjoy so much money when I had to work all the time. I would really have to think about that. I figured God, in his subtle way, was telling me to bail out.

Fulfilled greed has a way of inducing euphoria. The more I made, the more I wanted. The more I wanted, the more I made. And the more convicted I was that all of this was from God. Why me? Perhaps to reward me for my faith. The way God rewarded Job for his faithfulness. After the meanness and pain of the divorce several years before, he was finally taking care of me.

By January, silver had climbed to $50 an ounce. Gold was at $800, and everybody was saying it would reach $1000 before the Dow did. On paper, my net profits exceeded $300,000. I began thinking in earnest about retirement.

Then the unthinkable happened. The inevitable happened. The bubble burst. The metals markets went into free fall. Each day they were "locked down limit"—the price dropped as far as the markets would allow, and trading was suspended. I was on a falling elevator, watching the floors pass by yet not able to step off.

I really didn't want off. I had staying power. I had built this thing from scratch. I knew it was just a matter of time before the elevator started its ascent again. And I could get out if I needed to. There were ways.

I prayed fervently. "God, if you want me out at $40, just give me a sign. Send me a postcard. I'll do whatever you say. Though I'm sure you don't want me to realize any of these paper losses when you're planning on bringing this market back." "Well, Lord, if you want me to sell at $29, just give me the word. I stand ready to do your will." "Okay, Lord, $19 is really testing my faith. Tell me if you want me to sell."

Two weeks after the fall began, it was all over. I was out. Not because God had told me to get out. He had remained amazingly quiet. I got out because I had no choice. Automatic triggers were activated, and I was out. With nothing. Zilch. Zero. Zip. *Nada*. Nothing. I had lost it all.

I was so angry with God. What kind of sadistic game was this? Why had he stopped blessing me all of a sudden? Hadn't I constantly asked him to help me make a decision?

Well, yes. But only after I had spent months working

solo. And my deep convictions of God's guidance came only after I was hundreds of thousands of dollars to the good. At the same time I was convicted of his guidance, I was also impressed by my own wisdom and prowess.

To my credit, immature as I was, I do remember looking at biblical examples. I did wonder how the apostles felt when they saw their number, handpicked by the Master himself, whittled, pared, and hacked down by crucifixions, beheadings, and beast games. And I wondered how they felt when they were in the cell, just before they were killed for Christ's cause. Were they pleading for God to take the cup from their hand? Did they beg him to make them the exception? And how much money did those guys make, anyway? Surely if God had intended for his best and brightest to be blessed with high incomes, wouldn't he have padded their pockets a little?

Such moments of lucid thought were few and far between, overshadowed by my own grief and shame. I had bragged so much. And lost so much. And God had let me down. I shook my fist at him. I stomped my feet. I threw a tantrum.

But God is nothing if not patient.

He let me vent my pain. Then he put it all in perspective.

A week after the devastating loss, I discovered a small lump on one of my testicles. I was alarmed, sure it hadn't been there six weeks earlier when I had reversed my vasectomy. I called the surgeon who had operated on me to see what he thought. He thought he wanted to see me. Today. Could I be there in an hour?

Mary and I both have medical backgrounds; she is a critical care nurse, and I was trained as a combat medic. We were prepared for the absolute worst when we stepped into his office.

After a brief examination, the doctor said, "Mr. Toombs, testicular cancer is rare among men your age, but its effects can be devastating. There is a very high mortality rate. I would prefer to have a second opinion by a cancer specialist at the Medical School." He made the call, and our next stop was the cancer specialist.

He was equally grave. "It is important that we operate, quickly."

"When did you want to do it?" I asked. "Next week?"

"How about tomorrow morning?"

"Tomorrow morning? No way. I've got too much to do. There are things I have to wrap up at the office." I hadn't yet accepted that I might have a life-threatening disease.

"Wednesday then."

"It's only Monday!"

"Mr. Toombs, time is of the essence. While the likelihood that you have cancer is small, the cost of delaying, if you do, is too high. If I could operate this afternoon, that would be my choice."

Swallowing hard, I looked at Mary. Tears of fear and concern rimmed her eyes. I could feel myself becoming numb. "We'll do it Wednesday," I agreed.

I asked my good friend Pete Leininger, a urologist, to stand in during the surgery in case any critical decisions were required while I was under the anesthesia. Pete knew of our desire for children and had been my guide during the whole process of having the vasectomy reversed. I probably owe my two sons to him.

That night we called our home Bible study group together to pray.

"You know, a week ago I was whining and moaning about having lost all that money in precious metals," I explained. "Now that seems such a long time ago. It is so unimportant compared with what we are facing now. God has a way of allowing things to happen so our attention gets focused back on the important things, doesn't he?"

We prayed for some time, Mary and I and those good friends in the Lord. I began to see with clarity how foolish my previous months' preoccupation with wealth had been. I had been majoring in minors. And I had failed to get the point, even after it had all been stripped out of my hands. I had still looked at the money as if it were the most important thing in the world. It wasn't even close.

Asking Pete to assist in the surgery was a good decision. At two or three critical points his calm intervention stayed the surgeon's hand from a more radical course. I came out of the surgery as whole as I went in, save for one small, benign cyst, which I was happy to be rid of.

And I got something extra. A three-inch scar across my abdomen that no one sees except Mary and me. Yet for me it is as much an Ebenezer as the original. Remember the story? Samuel, a prophet and one of Israel's last judges, had been empowered to lead Israel to victory against their ancient enemies, the Philistines. After the decisive battle, Samuel set up a rock between Mizpah and Shen and named it Ebenezer, "stone of help," as a memorial to "God the Rock" who had helped Israel in their fight against the Philistines.[1]

My scar is my memorial. Every time I see it I am reminded of God's grace and the constant need to check my priorities. Sometimes I get bogged down in my own personal Philistia. I begin focusing on the wrong things, majoring in minors again. But then I'll take a shower and there it is. Good old Ebenezer. Right where we left him. And then I remember. The important things.

CLIFFHANGER

Everyone must submit himself to the governing authorities, for there is no authority except that which God has established. The authorities that exist have been established by God. Consequently, he who rebels against the authority is rebelling against what God has instituted, and those who do so will bring judgment on themselves.

ROMANS 13:1-2

On his robe and on his thigh he has this name written:
KING OF KINGS AND LORD OF LORDS.

REVELATION 19:16

MAYBE IT WAS THE FACT that we were on vacation. Or extra high testosterone levels. Maybe it was a boyish spirit of adventure. Or just plain, old-fashioned rebellion.

Whatever was behind it, violating the rules almost cost us our lives.

"Us" were my friend Jim and I. Jim is a physician and the CEO of a medical manufacturing company. At the time I was the vice president of marketing. We had been exhibiting at the Rocky Mountain Neurosurgical Society meeting at Jackson Lake Lodge, just outside Yellowstone National Park. Jim's Cecelia, and Mary were our demonstration models.

The meeting had been quite successful, and we had the opportunity to reward ourselves with a one-day sweep through Yellowstone, something I would not normally recommend. God created the wonders of Yellowstone over millions of years: geysers, geothermal paint pots, bubbling sulfur pools, and waterfalls that literally take your breath away. And he chose to spread it over an area almost three times the size of Rhode Island. It deserves more of your time than a mere day.

But our timing was perfect. We entered the park one day ahead of the bumper-to-bumper RVs that have come to characterize the nation's oldest national park. And we did almost a complete circuit in our one day. We experienced sensory overload.

Our tongues were in our cheeks as we spoke of being nature-sated. "Well, well, well. Another magnificent waterfall." (Yawn) "And look. Another array of crystal clear, multicolored pools of almost boiling water. Ooops. Time to go. There's another thundering waterfall just ahead." (Sigh)

It really wasn't fair to the park. This is an area to linger over, to reflect on the powers and ingenuity of our Creator. It is hard to conceive of the mind that could itself conceive of such beauteous wonders.

Along with not being fair to the park and its Creator, our whirlwind tour also left us hungering for bigger and bigger thrills. Especially us guys.

That's what got us into trouble. And almost cost Jim and me our lives.

We stopped at the top of the trail leading to the Great Falls of the Yellowstone. There were four hundred thirty-six steps leading down to we-didn't-know-where and signs warning those who were pregnant or who had a heart condition to think twice before beginning their descent. The four intrepid explorers had already seen several magnificent waterfalls so we weren't sure we needed to see this one. Four hundred thirty-six steps was a lot of steps. San Antonio rests at an altitude of only about seven hundred feet above sea level, Yellowstone at over seven thousand feet. The air, what there was of it, was thin for us flatlanders. Would we go for it? This called for a quick powwow. The women were unsure but willing to follow our lead. The men checked to see if anyone was pregnant or had a heart condition—we weren't and didn't. So on we pushed past the warning signs.

Not another human being passed us during our journey to the bottom of the steps. Continuing on, we found ourselves in a covered pavilion overlooking the magnificent falls. We were still over a hundred yards away, but the sight was breathtaking. Several stories above us, to our left, the Yellowstone River simply stopped in midair, making an abrupt detour to the canyon floor another hundred feet below our position. Even from a distance we could sense the power as the great cataract sent mist halfway up the falls from the gyrating waters below. A snow-covered promontory obstructed our view of the bottom of the falls, but off to our right the river reappeared as a boiling cacophony of white water before it disappeared into the mouth of the canyon a thousand feet downstream from the falls itself.

The pavilion was so far away it was as if we were seeing a movie of the waterfall instead of the real thing. Jim and I craved more. We looked over the pine log railing and evaluated the ground below sloping gently down to the falls. Ignoring the National Park Service signs forbidding us to go any further, and the clear warning of our wives, we looked at each other, grinned, and slipped our legs over the railing and walked out to the promontory.

The closer we got, the louder the falls became. And the more we could feel the vibrations in the ground. When we got to within about twelve feet of the edge of the river, the ground seemed to churn beneath our feet. The cold mist stung my face. The cascading water mesmerized us as we watched individual gouts of water slowly twist and turn, falling foot by foot to disappear below the snowy edge in front of us. It was truly awesome. The power. The raw power thundered through our bodies. I could feel it in my chest, in my lungs, with every breath. The mountain seemed to breathe for me.

"That's incredible!" Jim said. "It's like it resonates in every cell in your body." Spoken like a doctor, I thought. And right on target.

"Guess we better head back," I said. "The women are probably worrying, don't you think?"

"No doubt," he said, looking downriver. "Hey, let's go this way. It looks a little more interesting."

Interesting was an understatement. The flat we were on in the middle of the hill rose to about a forty-five degree angle as it swept on around the pavilion up the rise. In the opposite direction it terminated a couple of hundred feet below at the water's edge. The entire expanse of iron red hillside was covered with tiny fractured fragments of granite. And the only vegetation was an occasional clump of long, stringy grass and several limbs protruding from a single, scraggly, water-starved bush a little higher up the hill. The bush was on the downstream side of the pavilion far from the mist of the falls. If we could get to it, we had an easy climb uphill to the pavilion.

"Looks doable. Can you make it in those?" I questioned, pointing at Jim's shoes. They were low quarters with a rippled sole that didn't look very flexible. I was wearing well-broken-in, high-topped, combat boots, courtesy of my generous Uncle Sam.

"They're not the best, but they'll do."

I nodded and went first. The gravel was treacherous. It was like trying to walk on a hill coated with ball bearings. Fortunately there were small, half-buried rocks in the hillside that gave us a place to get a foothold. Until we were within ten feet of the scraggly bush. Then there was only one flat rock about half the size of a saucer, and a single clump of grass. I stepped onto the high side of the rock, digging my toes into the hard earth above it. It gave slightly, then held. I brought over my right foot, found purchase, then pushed off, reaching for the clump of grass with my left hand. My left foot was on ball bearings. Below was a raging torrent of white water. Now I was spread-eagled on the side of the mountain.

As I clung to the hillside, the conversation we had earlier with the ranger in the Smokey Bear hat came back to me. Jim asked him if anyone ever fell into the boiling river.

"We lose two or three a year," he said. "Lost a twelve-year-old girl last year, right at the close of the season."

"Lost her?" I asked.

"Yes. Never did find her body. But that's not unusual. That river beats 'em to pieces."

"Has anybody ever survived?" I asked.

"I'm sure they have. But I've never heard of it."

My hand caught the clump of grass, and my left foot found a small prominence as I pulled myself over to a safe place.

"How was it?" Jim wondered aloud.

"Pretty hairy," I said. "But you can make it. Just make sure you step where I stepped. This gravel is like trying to climb on marbles."

"Gotcha."

Jim stepped out on faith in his clunky shoes and found the flat rock. He brought his other foot over and then the unthinkable happened. The flat rock began to slide. Whenever he shifted his weight to step off, the rock gave way some more. My eyes grew wider as Jim hugged the red hillside.

"I can't get back," he said. "And I can't come forward. I'm stuck."

I thought about the warning sign we had so glibly bypassed.

"How much do you weigh?" I asked.

"180."

I'm only 135. That's why I made it and he was stuck. That extra 45 pounds.

"Hold on, Jim. I'm going to grab the limb of that bush. It may support us so I can swing you over here. Why don't you pray."

"I am praying."

I prayed, too—a short prayer. No time for eloquence.

"Do you think you can do it?" There was concern on Jim's face. Maybe even fear.

"No sweat. If this…bush holds." I stretched to reach the brittle bush and worked my hand to the base where the branches were thicker and less likely to snap. But the roots of the plant were not deep. The whole thing might pull out of the ground with our combined weights on it.

"Okay, I've got it. Grab my hand. And when you swing over, step on my foot. I've already got a pretty good bite. It ought to take the extra weight." I sounded more optimistic than I really was.

"Lord, help us," I prayed as I reached out my hand.

Jim grabbed it with his outstretched hand. I watched his right foot as he put all his weight on it, moving his left foot towards my planted boot. The rock slipped more. I hugged the hillside with my cheek, my chest, my thighs. Every possible part of my body was making intimate contact with Yellowstone.

Jim's weight was frightening. I could feel the branch stretching and cracking and my body beginning to slide. In my mind I saw the two of us slipping down the hill, fingers outstretched in a futile attempt to stop our descent into the raging white water below.

He pushed off, pulling hard on my arm as he reached for the safety of the hillside just beyond me. The flat rock scuttled down the hill, disappearing over the edge of the river into the foaming whiteness.

As soon as Jim's weight was off my arm and my foot, I collected my body and clambered up to the bush where Jim was waiting. "Thank you, Lord," I breathed, dusting the granite shards out of the soft flesh of my cheek.

"Amen to that," Jim said. "I didn't know if we were going to make it or not."

"I know what you mean. Did you see that rock you were standing on?"

"It never made a splash. It just disappeared into the water, like we would have."

"I guess they knew what they were doing when they stuck those signs up," I offered.

He smiled sheepishly and agreed.

Jim and I talked about that adventure years later. We talked about how exciting it had been. And how foolish we had been to go past the warning signs.

Going past the warning signs seems to be a metaphor for my life. I have always been aggressive. I have considered the word no to be a challenge, an obstacle to circumnavigate. The question has always been, how could I find a way around it?

That strategy served me well in school to help me learn. When teachers taught things that didn't make sense to me, I challenged them. They either clarified the situation for me, or, more rarely, if they had made a mistake, they changed their position.

In business when the rules seemed too restrictive, I challenged them. When a television production facility told me a shot or effect wasn't possible, I found a way around it. If a printer or graphic designer said we couldn't produce what I had conceived, I pushed until we found a way around it. It was like a game. They raised obstacles; I found ways around them.

So long as I knew what rule was getting in my way, I would try to find a legitimate way around it. That is all fine and good when I'm playing a game or when I am making a commercial or doing a business deal. But the attitude behind that life strategy can breed a devil-may-care arrogance. And there are times when the devil cares very much.

Such as when I violate the commands of Christ by going around the rules of the authorities who serve at his will. When I rebel at those rules, there can be the devil to pay, whether I am caught or not. Even if the consequences don't show up in this physical world, there are always spiritual repercussions when we break duly ordained rules.

I still live on the edge to a large extent, (though age has a way of moderating some of that behavior). But now I try to be aware of the consequences of coloring outside the lines. Now I make more careful distinctions between the rules established by legal authority and those established for convenience. Because now I understand that Jesus is the King of all kings. He is the Lord of all lords on earth or in heaven. All the kings and all the lords serve at his will. They make rules at his will, even if I disagree with them. So, if I violate those rules, I am offending the King of kings and the Lord of lords. I am challenging his authority and putting myself on the same side as the devil.

And that's a downhill slide to oblivion.

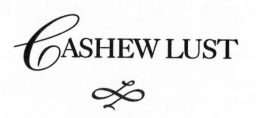CASHEW LUST

"Love your neighbor as yourself."

MATTHEW 22:39

CASHEW LUST, that's what it was. Otherwise I would never have done it.

I had left home in my typical no-time-to-spare fashion. On the way to church the urge came over me. Cashews. I wanted some. Not just a little bitty bag—a whole can. But cashews are expensive. Especially at convenience store prices.

Suddenly I remembered the long lost Diamond Shamrock cash stamp books I had found in my car just the week before. Together the two of them were worth six bucks. The cashews were mine!

I pulled into the Shamrock on Hildebrand. I had twenty-three minutes. I ran inside.

I scanned the Cornnuts and cheese crackers. No nuts.

"Ma'am," I called across the store. "Where are your salted nuts?"

"On the other side of the aisle," she waved.

Oh, man! I'd already been over there. All they had were the little cellophane tubes—$1.99 for a dabble. And an off-brand. Not high quality. Not what I had in mind. But all I could find. I had nineteen minutes as I grabbed a tube and headed for the counter.

First I dropped my stamp books on the counter. They would be useless on such a small purchase. Then the nuts. I fumbled in my wallet for the cash as she said, "Ninety-nine cents, please."

Ninety-nine cents? I thought they were $1.99! Maybe she knew something I didn't know. Maybe I didn't care. Maybe I just saved a dollar at Shamrock's expense. That would teach them to carry the right-sized packages! And get a good brand while they were at it!

I pocketed the change, grabbed my cashews, and dashed to my car. Fourteen minutes. I felt a stab of guilt.

The nuts were half-gone as I turned onto the access road of I-10. Guilt twisted my insides as it pierced my body. If I hadn't already eaten most of them and if I had more than eleven minutes to get to church, I would go back and give her the stupid dollar. I still had $6 worth of stamps...somewhere. *I left them on the counter!*

I saw the turnoff to the right just before I got on the expressway. If I took a couple of back roads, I could make it back there in just a few minutes, get my $6 worth of stamps, and get to church only a few minutes late. The folks in Divorce Recovery would understand. They were probably going to be late anyway, I rationalized.

I opened the door talking. "Do you have my stamps?" I asked, polite strain in my voice.

The clerk looked at me as if she had never seen me before. Then a small light of recognition flashed across her face, followed by a look of panic. "I thought they were hers!" she said.

"Hers whose?"

"The lady. She picked them up. I thought they were hers."

That good-for-nothing thief! The woman behind me saw me leave them and picked them up. She knew they weren't hers. She stole them. She stole them! She stole my stamps.

I was fuming as I got back in the car. My hand stung from slamming it on the counter in angry frustration.

"I can't believe some people!" I muttered. "She saw me put them on the counter. She saw me leave. She was probably hoping I would leave them. What a jerk!"

And then it hit me. She had done exactly what I had done. Only she did it to me, not to the nameless, faceless owners of Diamond Shamrock, Inc.

I had broken the second law. It wasn't the $1...or the $6. It was the fact that I had done to someone else the very thing that enraged me when it happened to me. I had not done to my neighbor as I would have had my neighbor do to me. Diamond Shamrock is my neighbor as sure as the person next door.

But I hadn't really considered that as I rushed to cash in on the clerk's mistake. Cashew lust and opportunistic gain had blinded me and kept me from seeing a truth I had not only pledged to live my life by and to teach to my children, but had this very day taught in Bible class!

My howls of indignation came as the Holy Spirit whacked me across the behind, spiritually speaking of course. It was truly an act of love on his part, and I praise God that he brought my sin to my attention almost immediately. As soon as I calmed down and stopped throwing my anger at the lady who took my stamps, I could see that we were guilty of the same thing. I remembered the passage in Proverbs that talks about God's chastening love. And it seemed truer to me than ever before: "Because the Lord disciplines those he loves, as a father the son he delights in."[1]

I decided it's good to have my father delight in me enough to get my attention when I mess up. Even when it hurts. And while there is an enormous difference between my heavenly father and the manager of the gas station, I found they could both forgive the same mistake.

THE PRICE OF ADMISSION

We know that we are children of God, and that the whole world is under the control of the evil one.

1 JOHN 5:19

I LOVE MOVING PICTURES. I'm one of the first of the video generation. Television and I spent our infancies together. Our first set had a seven-inch screen, and I remember Mom and Dad inviting the neighbors down to watch it. The house was so small they put the television in the front window, and everybody gathered outside on the front lawn to watch the dancing black and white images.

As a teenager, I memorized *TV Guide*. Tell me what you were watching, and I could tell you the night, time, channel, network, who the stars were, and in most cases I could hum a few bars of the theme song. I liked TV a lot. I liked the flickering images so much I even got my undergraduate degree in radio, TV, and film. Transferring my love for television to film, I became a student of film.

I believed it was vital for me to see the latest movies. Especially the important ones. And the controversial ones.

I remember how "with it" and mature I felt in college when I would see movies for class that others saw for fun. The more outrageous the film, or the more obscure, the better I liked it. *Easy Rider* was an eloquent study in the clash of traditional values with the new counterculture. *Who's Afraid of Virginia Woolf* was like seeing inside the boozing, bloated marriage of Burton and Taylor. The foreign films of Fellini and Kurosawa were difficult, with their subtitles. But none was more haunting and more challenging than Bergman's *The Seventh Seal*, which climaxed in a medieval chess match between the tall, austere, and lordly protagonist (played by Max von Sydow) and Death himself.

Becoming a Christian had little impact on my movie-viewing habits. After all, I was already three years into my program when I was baptized. My course had been set. But that was a milder time for movies. The scenes and the language were more fitting to family audiences then, and films made for young people were never challenged on their content, at least not in this country.

Somewhere along the way, though, things changed. The movie-rating system was inaugurated by Hollywood to forestall censorship from Washington. Four-letter words became standard fare, even in PG movies. In 1939 *Gone With the Wind* had only one curse word in it. Last year, a major Oscar contender had nearly four hundred. Now everyone curses in movies, even small children. Hollywood seems to delight in letting innocents blurt out curse words, the more coarse the better. The purpose? They say it's reality—that's the way kids talk today. I think it's pandering. They want to shock and titillate and establish rapport with the youthful audience.

And nudity, once restricted to quick flashes of partially concealed female breasts in X-rated films, now finds its way into PG-13 movies. R-rated movies usually include at least one, often gratuitous, steamy sex scene.

The sexual interactions are blatant. Whereas subtlety and suggestion were the norm in films even into the seventies, now the relationships are raw and filled with power and passion. Images are anything but subtle as hands and mouths grab hungrily for flesh. And the scenes are increasingly perverted, including sadomasochism, homosexuality, and multiple partners.

And they are increasingly accessible to our children. In fact, our kids can see aspects of human sexuality in the movies which some of us would never, ever find acceptable to discuss with them...or anybody else, including our spouses.

While the depiction of sexuality seems more and more pornographic, perhaps our real concern should be violence. You can see...and will see...graphic examples of murder, torture, molestation, dismemberment, brutality, cruelty, and general mayhem in lots of movies aimed at younger, impressionable audiences. Little is left to the imagination as body parts and gore go flying across the movie screen. There's even a genre of B-class movies that specializes in such stuff—the "splatter pictures."

But kids also encounter obscene and explicit violence in A films aimed at children: movies like *Terminator II*, and *Robocop*, and even *Batman Returns*. And how do I know they are aimed at younger children? Who clamors for the action figures and other toys licensed around these movies? And why would the toymakers create toys unless the movies created a demand for them? Market demand is not created by parents telling their kids about the movies they see, but by the kids seeing the movies themselves.

So what's the point for today's Christian, me specifically?

The point is, as the cartoon character Pogo said, "I has seen the enemy and he is us!"

You see, I watch those movies. And so do a lot of you. We are the market. We supply the demand for what Hollywood creates. Why? Perhaps because the degradation of the product has been gradual and we have tended to dismiss it. Maybe because the images are pleasing to my eyes. And I rationalize. I tell myself it's okay. They are only movies. It's just fantasy. It's entertainment. I can handle it. Whom does it hurt, anyway?

I found out the other day.

I'm embarrassed to tell you the movie I saw. But you can't appreciate what I'm going to say until you know the movie. It was *Basic Instincts* with Michael Douglas. His father, Kirk Douglas, was one of my favorite actors when I was a kid. Son Michael has all his dad's charisma, and probably more talent.

Before the curtain ever went up, I was having second thoughts and conscience pangs. I didn't really know much about the movie except that it was a thriller, had gotten good reviews, had some sensational scenes in it, and starred Michael Douglas. But I was still uneasy.

As we made our way to our seats, I saw a woman in the crowd I vaguely knew, but I couldn't place her. She looked at me strangely as I took my seat. Then the theater darkened, and my attention was focused on the screen.

The movie is basically about a policeman in search of a female murderer. We know she's female because in the opening scene we see her without any clothes on preparing to have relations with a man tied to a very ritzy bed in a very ritzy bedroom. In the process, they manage to perform several deviant behaviors, the most deviant being his brutal murder by her at the most climactic moment of the scene. (Pun fully intended.)

I couldn't believe what I was seeing on the screen. And I couldn't believe I was still sitting there. But the movie was successful in the Hollywood sense. It was riveting. It was dramatic. It had great production values. And it was disgusting.

I continued to watch the movie, telling myself, "It will get better. Perhaps there is something socially redeeming. Look for it." With this new task I clicked into my critical mode. I watched every scene with the eye of a critic. But I was disappointed. There really wasn't anything socially redeeming about the movie. There was violence, homosexuality, murder, deviant sexual behavior, bisexuality, casual sexual relationships, contempt for other people, a general lack of integrity—and it was all presented as somewhat normal in the context of the characters' lives.

I watched the whole movie...and felt embarrassed when I left...and more than a little soiled.

Then I saw the woman again. The one I couldn't place.

The look she gave me was a look I will never forget—a look of betrayal and disappointment. I couldn't understand it. Not until I got to church a week later.

A friend approached me and told me I had been seen at the movie by the woman in question. My gut tightened. I felt as if I had been caught. He reminded me of who she was. She was a woman I had told about Jesus in a chance meeting. I had invited her to church. Where we don't behave as people in the world behave. Where we don't behave like the people she had known.

Paul says we are Christ's ambassadors, as though God were making his appeal toward reconciling the world to him directly through us.[1] Partly for that reason, God demands that the leaders of his church be above reproach.[2]

If I had been working for the government as an ambassador, I might have been recalled for that incident. My behavior certainly wasn't above reproach, neither in her eyes nor in mine.

She knew what we were doing was inconsistent with a Christian life. So did I. And because I was a Christian—and a Christian leader at that—she expected more discretion, more discernment, perhaps more self-control. And she expected a higher level of moral behavior from me. She certainly expected me to act differently than she did. But I didn't.

She never came back to church. I'm not sure why, but I have to think the movie incident played a part.

And I never got to tell her anything more about Jesus.

I didn't get to tell her about his kindness and his respect and his saving grace.

I didn't get to tell her about his love.

And I didn't get to tell her how he forgives people like her...and me.

THE BLAME GAME

"Have you eaten from the tree that I commanded you not to eat from?"

The man said, "The woman you put here with me—she gave me some fruit from the tree, and I ate it."

GENESIS 3:11-12

"YOU'RE GONNA HAVE a great day today," I told my son Michael as we pulled into the church parking lot.

"Yeah, Dad. I've been wanting to go to the water park all week."

We walked into the foyer and looked around. Nobody was there yet. Michael looked anxious so I said, "The paper said you would be leaving at 9:30. It's only 8:55, so you have a little wait. Besides, the van is out there waiting for you. Let's go sit in my office until it's time to go."

He still looked worried so I added, "And if you want, you can go check the back parking lot just in case they are waiting there." He shrugged, and we went into my office.

At 9:30 the alarm on my computer beeped, and we went into the foyer. Still nobody. I looked outside. The van was gone.

I looked at Michael. He looked at me. My stomach took a wrong turn as I turned to talk to the secretaries.

"Is Doris Bruner here?"

"She left," said one of the secretaries.

"With a bunch of kids?"

In her best, stern, mother voice the secretary said, "She said to be here at 9:00. You blew it, Dad. They're on their way to Splashtown. Too bad." She smiled, and it was all I could do to keep from giving her an unministerial punch in the smile.

"Thanks for the affirmation," I snarled over my shoulder.

"Go down I-10 to 35 and then exit Splashtown Drive," she yelled as I turned away.

"I don't need directions," I snapped back. I knew exactly where the water park was. It was five minutes from my house. The church was twenty minutes in the opposite direction.

As we got to the car, Michael asked, "What time is it, Dad?"

"Get in the car, Michael."

"What time is it, Dad?" he repeated as he was opening the car door.

"Get in the car, Michael. I'll tell you when you get in the car." I might not have control of the situation, but I could at least have control of my son!

As his door slammed, I said, "It's 9:30, the time you were *supposed* to leave." Gravel flew and rubber burned as I screeched out of the church parking lot. I sped all the way to the interstate. Just let a cop catch me, I thought.

Where had they been? Doris is like one of those little white tornadoes—constant energy in motion. Whether she's taking sandwiches to the homeless under the downtown bridges or ramrodding a group of fourth graders, usually you can hear her all over the church building. Why was she so quiet today? And why hadn't they been in the chapel where they usually wait?

"I bet they were in the parking lot where you told me to look, Dad," said Michael, looking guilty.

Most of me ignored this subtle confession, though a small part held on to it, ready to use it to teach him a lesson at the proper moment: "When I tell you to do something, son...." But not now. Now I was still blaming the secretaries for rubbing my nose in my mistake. Didn't they see Michael with me? Didn't they know why he was there? The secretary as much as admitted she did when she told me Doris had taken the kids to Splashtown. What was she thinking? What were the other women thinking? It wasn't my fault. We had been there.

As we got to Splashtown, I thought, This is the last time I take the kids anywhere. Mary never gives me the right information. If I ever do this again, she's going to have to give me all the details in writing. In fact, I won't do it unless she gives me the original paper. Hummph!

Then my son said, "They should have waited on us. They better not be swimming yet!"

I immediately became irritated with him. Here he was acting like a child again. When would he learn to take responsibility for his own behavior? Never one to miss an opportunity to teach my children, I lobbed a guilt grenade, "Michael, we might not have missed them if we had checked that back parking lot."

That was when it struck me, like one of those Elmer Fudd cartoons. Elmer is chasing Bugs Bunny through a hollow log. Bugs gets out first and turns the log so Elmer runs off a cliff. For a split second, old Fudd realizes he's been had. He feels like a sucker. He even turns into a candy sucker, just before he plummets earthward. If I had been a cartoon character, I would have turned into a sucker there in the front seat of the van.

I was pulling an Adam. "It was that woman YOU gave me, Lord." I was pointing my blame finger at anyone unlucky enough to get in the way. First I aimed at Doris. Then at the secretaries. Then I blamed my wife. And finally my son. Now, here was Michael doing the same thing, just as he'd seen his old man perform. He was a real chip off the old block.

It's painful enough just to see my mistakes, God. Do you have to show them to me through my son like this?

My stomach churned with this sudden realization. I stopped Michael. "It wasn't their fault," I said. "And it wasn't your fault. We made a mistake. No, I made a mistake. I had the original sheet Doris gave you with all the information about today's activities, and I threw it away. I thought I could remember everything I needed to know. But I didn't. It's nobody's fault but mine, Michael."

"It's nobody's fault but mine." Hard words to say. They

stuck in my throat. My face burned with shame for a moment. Then I realized my anger was gone. My anger with Doris was gone. And so was my anger with the secretaries, and Michael, and Mary. And my anger with myself was gone. My confession had completely taken away my anger. Incredible. And then I noticed the shame was gone.

As I wrote this, I wondered what it would be like to let someone else read what a fool I had been. Forget all you readers I'll probably never meet. I decided to check it out with a tough audience. I asked my other son, Geoffrey, to read it.

After he finished, I asked him how he felt, reading about his dad making a mistake.

"I don't know," he replied, wrinkling his nose.

"What do you mean?"

"Well, I like it, but I thought you were perfect, Dad."

Perfect. Don't I want to be perfect? In my kids' eyes? In my friends' eyes? In the eyes of other Christians? Don't I want to be seen as someone who has it all together? Don't you?

I find it really tough to accept and admit my own weaknesses. My tendency is to protect myself, to defend my image. Even though I want to be vulnerable and real to people, I don't want to disappoint them. So I'm tempted to protect the myth that I'm a good man, even if I have to shove the responsibility for my mistakes off on someone else.

But here's the good news: I wasn't called to be perfect.

And when I realize I wasn't called to be perfect, except in Jesus, it frees me up. Jesus is the expiation of my sin. "Expiation" is one of those four dollar religious words that means he paid the full price my sin earned. And sin earns only one thing: death.[1] Death is the wage of any sin, including the sin of not accepting responsibility. Or trying to blame someone else for my shortcomings.

Exposing my sins to myself is hard to do. I can't do it by myself. I need the help of the Holy Spirit. Otherwise my sins sneak up on me and bite me when I'm not looking. I want to blame them on someone else. But if I get away with blaming someone else, I don't grow. My pride does, but I don't. I can't grow as long as I believe in the myth of my own goodness. So I must become myth-informed.

And I must accept responsibility for my imperfections and my goofs. Even when they happen at the expense of my parental pride. All that leads me to maturity in Christ.

Michael did have a great day at the waterpark. When we arrived, the waiting area was flush with fourth graders chomping and stomping for the place to open. As often happens, my flub was nowhere near as catastrophic as it seemed. The real drama took place inside me and between my son and me. God had used an opportunity to teach me something very important about myself. And by showing me my weakness, he helped me become stronger.[2]

DOLORES

"Then he will say to those on his left, 'Depart from me, you who are cursed, into the eternal fire prepared for the devil and his angels. For I was hungry and you gave me nothing to eat, I was thirsty and you gave me nothing to drink, I was a stranger and you did not invite me in, I needed clothes and you did not clothe me, I was sick and in prison and you did not look after me.'

"They also will answer, 'Lord, when did we see you hungry or thirsty or a stranger or needing clothes or sick or in prison, and did not help you?'

"He will reply, 'I tell you the truth, whatever you did not do for one of the least of these, you did not do for me.'"

MATTHEW 25:41-45

HER VOICE SQUEAKED over the phone like Styrofoam being cut with a dull knife. It made my teeth hurt.

"Hallow? I'm the lady Allen told you about. My husband hasn't gotten paid for two months, and they're gonna turn off our lights. Did y'all collect any money for us?"

Desperation.

Defeat.

Manipulation.

Whining.

I wanted to talk to this lady about as much as I wanted to stick my tongue in a light socket. Whiny people drive me nuts.

I put on my best ministerial demeanor. "Hello, Mrs. Welch. Why don't you tell me what's going on."

"Didn't Allen tell you? I don' wanna repeat what he said. Tell me what he said so I don' repeat nothin'." High. Shrill. It was all I could do not to cut her off and pass her on to one of the other ministers.

With forced pleasantness I said, "He really didn't tell me much more than there had been some foul-up with your husband's pay and you were not able to pay your bills. Why don't you tell me what's happened."

"He din't tell you nothin'? Well," she took a deep breath and launched into her sad story, "my husband works at the air base and they got his pay messed up and he hasn't gotten no paycheck for two months an' if I don't pay the light bill they're gonna shut off the lights tomorrow an' I can't get no job 'cause I got a retarded daughter at home I gotta take care of an' nobody helps us with nothin' an' my husband's got a heart condition an' he couldn't work much last year so our bills just stacked up and stacked up an' now his pay is messed up an' I don't know what I'm gonna do. If I don't pay them a hundred and fifty dollars tomorrow they're gonna shut off the lights so when Allen said the church could help I was so relieved."

I thought she would never breathe! Groan. My cynical side was having a field day with Dolores. My latent prejudices against weak, complaining people kept leaping to the front of my mind. I had visions of tough pioneers pulling themselves up by their bootstraps from prairie quagmires. And with that image I was contrasting Dolores. Poor, needy, whining Dolores. In the comparison sweepstakes she was coming up way short.

Yet my job was to help people like her. I felt guilty both for my mind-set and the disappointing message as I told her, "Mrs. Welch, it sounds like you've had a rough time of it. I told our Bible class about your problem this morning, and we took up a collection today to help you. But we didn't get much money. Certainly not $150."

There was silence as she processed what I had told her. The tiny balloon of hope that had buoyed her had been punctured. I could hear her spirits fall over the phone. But she quickly recovered. "Oh. Well…how much did you get? Maybe it will help."

"Maybe it will," I said. "We only collected $28." I was embarrassed by the small amount. "But I think there's another $30 or so in our class account."

Although we continued to talk for some time, my impressions of Dolores didn't improve. She kept peeling layer after layer of the onion of her despair, telling me of her pain and misery. As we finished the conversation, I made arrangements to meet her at the electric company the next day with a check for $58. Boy, was I looking forward to that! Not only would I be subjected to that voice face to face, but I had to drive across town to do it!

The next morning I drove for thirty minutes to meet with Dolores at the City Public Service offices. Pulling into a parking space I reflected on the meeting to come. I prayed that God would help my attitude toward this woman.

It was the right prayer at the right time. Because I was able to see Dolores in a new light. I knew her the instant I saw her: short, chubby, midthirties, but really ageless. Pain, fear, and hope were all mixed together on her face like colors on an artist's palette. Her shoulders were bowed by an invisible weight. Walking was an arduous chore for her. Her hips didn't seem to work right. My heart was stirred to compassion by the sight.

We talked about her retarded daughter and how she would never get better. She told me about her husband and how hard it had been to get the job as a janitor at the base and what a blessing it was that God had given it to them after his being out of work for so long.

As we talked face to face, Dolores began to change before my eyes. At first I wasn't sure what was happening. Then it hit me. She wasn't changing. I was. I was beginning to see what I had blinded myself to before. I was beginning to see Jesus in her.

It was humbling to have him wrapped in such a package. I was ashamed that I had almost failed to see him. And I was relieved and grateful that he had chosen to reveal himself to me before I damned myself in my haughty arrogance.

"Lord, when did we fail to help you when you were in need?"

"Get away from me, you hapless man. For I was hungry and you gave me nothing to eat, I was thirsty and you gave me nothing to drink, I was a stranger and you did not invite me in, I was Dolores and you treated me with contempt. Whatever you did not do for one of the least of these, you did not do for me."

We paid Dolores's electric bill and went our separate ways—she to the bus that would take her home, me to my car that would take me to the church building out by the Medical Center. It would be a wonderful ending to this story to tell you that encounter was a turning point in Dolores's life. I don't know if it was or not.

But it was in mine.

It was one of those "little" moments when I got the opportunity to apply the truth of God's word. I met her physical needs, and God—through her—met my spiritual need to see Jesus in someone less fortunate than myself.

He changed me in a fundamental way. Before Dolores I tended to be cynical and suspicious. I was afraid needy people like her were going to manipulate me and take advantage of me. I could think of dozens of reasons why we shouldn't help her, why she should get a job and help herself. Yet they were washed away by our face-to-face encounter. And because they were, because I allowed myself to behave in faith the way Jesus wanted, he began to change me.

I don't think I will ever be the same. Thank God.

$\mathcal{W}$HEN GOOD SAM BLOWS IT

"A man was going down from Jerusalem to Jericho, when he fell into the hands of robbers. They stripped him of his clothes, beat him and went away, leaving him half dead. A priest,...a Levite,...[and] a Samaritan, as he traveled, came where the man was; and when he saw him, he took pity on him....

"Which of these three do you think was a neighbor to the man who fell into the hands of robbers?"

SOMETIMES IT SEEMS as if my walk with Christ begins and ends at convenience stores.

The only reason I stopped there that night was to get gas. It wasn't on my usual route. Too far south of my home. But the neighborhood association meeting had ended later than I thought, and I knew this place would be open. So I pulled the old gold Camaro in beside the gas pumps, turned off the key, and went inside.

I looked around the store and saw only four people besides the night manager: a young black couple who seemed to be arguing, and two middle-aged Hispanic men. The manager was from somewhere in the Middle East.

The man at the front of the line was paying for his beer and pocketing his change when the argument at the rear of the store erupted into a string of obscenities. "I don't have to go nowhere with you!" the woman shouted.

He grabbed her arm.

"Let go of me. Get your hands off me! You don't own me. I don't have to go nowhere with you," she yelled, jerking away.

The man growled and tore himself away. He strode from the store, muttering as he left.

I watched. So did the other men. The woman looked up and made eye contact with the group at the cash register. She looked to be about sixteen or seventeen, really no more than a girl. Pretty and petite and bright-eyed, she reminded me of my daughters.

"Can one of you gentlemen help me?" she asked politely.

The other two customers shook their heads and turned away. The first man took his beer and left. The manager looked concerned but gently shook his head, too.

"What kind of help?" I asked.

"I need a ride home. Can you give me a ride home?"

"No, I don't think so." I turned away.

"But I don't have any way to get home. He left me stranded here."

"Why don't you call a cab?" I countered, turning back.

Her eyes got wide. "Oh, I don't have no money for no cab."

Of course not. This girl obviously didn't have fifteen dollars for cab fare. I didn't either. I'd left the house with no money, just a wallet full of credit cards.

"Well, call someone then. Call your folks."

"They don't have a car. Please, sir, can you help me?" Her eyes shifted from mine to the man behind the counter.

I turned back towards the counter, relieved to have her attention off me. "No, I cannot help you," the manager responded in clipped English, breaking eye contact and turning his attention back to the man in front of me.

I felt her presence behind me.

"Please, sir, can't you help me?" she pleaded.

"I...I can't take you home," I stammered, my resolve weakening. I've always been a sucker for damsels in distress. What would I want someone to do if this were my daughter?

"Where do you live?" I asked.

"On the other side of Blanco, near Colorado. It's not far."

She was right. It wasn't far. Just a few minutes away. Or a lifetime.

"Who was that guy? Your boyfriend?"

She laughed and tossed her head. "Him? No. We're just friends. He's not my boyfriend." Her smile was infectious.

"Well, that sure looked like a lover's spat," I said, weighing my options.

"No, we're just friends, Leroy and me."

"Did he leave? Or is he still hanging around here?"

"He better not be hanging around." There was heat in her eyes. "I told him to leave me alone." I admired her moxie.

"He didn't look too happy about it. Does he have a gun? Does he shoot people?" I felt guilty for asking, as if I'd just made a racial slur.

"Leroy? Naw, he don't have a gun. He wouldn't hurt nobody. Can you take me home, sir? Please?"

My heart said yes. My gut screamed no!

What would Jesus have done? I wondered.

"Okay, but I have to get gas first."

Air exploded from her chest as if she had been holding her breath. "Oh, thank you, sir. Nothing will happen. You'll see. Thank you so much."

The night manager shook his head as he took my money. "Probably not a Christian," I thought. I began to feel a little smug, maybe even self-righteous. That should have tipped me off.

We walked out to the gas island, and I let her in the passenger's side. I filled the tank with regular, hung up the nozzle, and got in the car. "Do I just go down Ashby here?" I asked, pointing.

"That's right."

As I pulled onto Ashby going west, I noticed a large, white car leave right behind me. Within half a block an uneasy feeling began taking over my stomach.

"Are you sure Leroy doesn't have a gun?" I asked, looking into the rearview mirror.

She glanced at my eyes, saw where I was looking, and jerked her head around to look at the lights behind us.

"Please don't stop, sir! Please don't stop! He ain't got no gun! Just don't stop!"

My gut was screaming at me now. "You idiot! I told you not to do this! Now what are you going to do?"

I remained calm. What was Leroy going to do? Didn't matter. He was in his car, I was in mine. I'd just find a cop. Then I realized with relief that the lights were pulling to the left. He was going to pass me.

Instead he came alongside, yelling and gesturing.

I rolled my window up and made the second major blunder of the evening. As I approached San Pedro Avenue, where I might have been able to find a cop, for some stupid reason I continued straight on Ashby. It was now almost ten o'clock and the street was pitch black and deserted as a cemetery. Even most of the houses were dark as tombs.

Fear was now the uninvited third occupant of the car.

Leroy pulled alongside again. I could see his mouth and arms moving, but my window shielded me from any sounds. My mind racing, I focused my attention on the road ahead, and Leroy dropped back in line. We would be coming up on the railroad tracks soon and then Blanco Street. I would turn left on Blanco. That would take me back into more familiar territory.

Again the car drew up on my left. This time I didn't even look in his direction but kept my eyes straight ahead.

So I never saw the flashes of light in his darkened car.

But I heard the three pops. And I felt my window disintegrate into a million pieces in one cataclysmic explosion.

My foot stomped the brake, and my hand shoved the gearshift into park, turned off the ignition, and pushed the girl into the floorboard in one sweeping movement. As my head vanished below the dash, I saw Leroy's taillights disappear over the hump of the railroad tracks.

For a long, long moment my body wouldn't work. It hadn't been shot; it just wouldn't work. And my mind wasn't much better. Fearing my reprieve might be short-lived and crazy Leroy might be heading back to finish me off, I sat up, glass tinkling into my lap. I shifted the car into drive. Nothing happened. I pressed the gas. Still nothing. A little dazed, I looked forward, surprised to see Leroy's lights again visible on the road ahead as he got to the bottom of the railroad tracks. Only seconds had passed. And I was in shock.

The keys! Where were the keys? In my hand. My right hand. Put them in the ignition. Put the gearshift into park. That's right. Now turn the key.

I popped the car into drive and surged over the railroad tracks. Incredibly, Leroy's speeding car was not more than a hundred yards in front of me. I floorboarded the accelerator and hit the Blanco intersection as his taillights disappeared to the right. I careened to the left. I was looking for a cop. Any cop.

Only moments later in the industrial area around Colorado Street, I found a police car in a parking lot. I pulled alongside him. "I've just been shot at." My voice was weak and shaky.

The cop put down his clipboard, opened his door, and sauntered over to the car. He looked in the window, shined the light on me, and then let it linger on my passenger. She was sitting in the seat, now, talking quietly to herself. His calmness and nonchalance filled me with fury.

"What seems to be the trouble? Anybody hurt?" He kept the light shining on her face.

After telling him the whole story, I calmed down somewhat, and we followed him to the police station to make a report. But the evening's surprises were not over yet.

At the station I was introduced to a detective, a man too big for his rumpled clothes. "You wanna come in and make a statement, Mr. Toombs?"

"Sure, but I need to call my wife first."

"That won't be necessary, sir." He had a gleam in his eye.

"What do you mean 'that won't be necessary'? I need to call her."

"I just mean you don't *have* to call her."

"I don't understand. Why wouldn't I want to call her? I just stopped for gas. I should have been home a long time ago."

"Go right ahead and call her, then. It's okay," he said with a smirk.

"What's going on here? What's this stuff about me not having to call her?"

"Well sir, when someone like you comes in with someone like her, it's usually because you've been doing some business. You know what I mean?" he winked.

"Business?" My chin hit my chest. "You mean you think she's a prostitute and I'm her…her…john?"

"Yessir, that is a normal reaction. And if you had been unfortunate enough to have been killed or wounded tonight, you can bet that is precisely how the papers would have played it."

I was outraged. "Hey. I was doing this girl a favor, giving her a ride home. I didn't know her boyfriend was anywhere around. She told me he had stranded her. I was just trying to be nice to her. Listen, I'm a minister. I'm happily married. I don't use prostitutes."

"Yessir. Now, can we fill out this report?"

He didn't believe me. He as much as accused me of being a whoremonger! I was outraged. And powerless.

As I filled out the report, one question kept ricocheting in my brain. Not a question, really. More of an accusation. Where was God during this whole fiasco? Why didn't he protect me?

Wait a minute. Who says he wasn't protecting me? Did I get hurt? Injured? Killed?

But why did this happen? I was just trying to do a good turn for someone in need. Isn't that what we are called to do? You can sure bet I'll never help anybody again!

Yeah, well, even if I do, maybe I'll have better judgment the next time. And on and on.

Have you ever noticed how often we question where

God is when we find ourselves in a fix? I think it comes up so often for me because of my imperfect understanding of God's will.

I get in trouble when I fail to balance my use of Scripture. I find a passage I like, I commit it to memory, and then I camp on it for a while. What I have is truth, but only partial truth, much like the blind men describing the elephant. Each of them fairly reported his perception of the elephant from the part he was touching. But none of them was able to get a broad overview to "see" what the whole beast was like.

I'm like that with God's word. Take these two verses, for instance:

Love your neighbor as yourself.[1]

I am sending you out like sheep among wolves. Therefore be as shrewd as snakes and as innocent as doves. [2]

I can hold on to "love your neighbor as yourself." Yet being "shrewd as snakes" tends to slip through my fingers like quicksilver.

If I had been shrewd as a snake, I, a married white man, might have thought two or three times before taking this stranger, this single, black woman, home at ten o'clock at night. I would have done what I could to help her, but I wouldn't have done what she herself could do. Isn't that the way God works with us? Rarely does he do for me what I can do for myself. It's part of that "free will" thing.

And, as a loving father, he allows me to suffer the consequences of my decisions, knowing that kind of experience is the best teacher of all.

But what of God? Where was he in this whole situation?

There's my arrogance rising up again. The question implies that, somehow, God is responsible for the bad things that happen to me. Which tends to discount both my own culpability, as well as what he has done to mitigate the consequences I have earned.

Because his hand was on me. By getting into the middle of a lover's spat, I could have easily been injured or killed. Instead I suffered nothing more than emotional distress and a fear of convenience stores for a few weeks. Yet rather than praising God for his goodness, I complained because it had happened at all. I didn't recognize that what occurred was a direct result of my bad decisions, not God's failure to intervene.

There's one final verse I stumbled over while I was writing this which seems to strike an appropriate balance.

> Like one who seizes a dog by the ears is a passer-by who meddles in a quarrel not his own.[3]

SATAN ON THE SKI SLOPES

In your anger do not sin and do not give the devil a foothold.

EPHESIANS 4:26-27

Love is patient, love is kind. It does not envy, it does not boast, it is not proud. It is not rude, it is not self-seeking, it is not easily angered, it keeps no record of wrongs.

1 CORINTHIANS 13:4-5

THERE WAS A PALLOR over the day our fourth day at Ski Apache in Ruidoso, New Mexico. I knew it as soon as my eyes opened that morning. I arose early, long before the rest of the family, to read my Bible and pray. I hadn't done that the entire vacation, yet. Something always got in the way. Like the morning paper, or making breakfast, or the fact that this was my vacation and I deserved to let go a bit.

The snow had been great—over ten inches of new snow the night we arrived. And the weather had been gorgeous for January. Bright, sunny, in the upper twenties. With no wind. But today there was a light cloud cover over the mountain, blocking the sun. I had forgotten to put on the bottoms to my long johns, so I was cold from the outset.

As we left the condo, I decided to let Rachel, my daughter, drive up the long, winding mountain road while I sat in the back with the boys. Before we reached the top, I was cracking jokes about Michael and me getting carsick.

For Michael it was no joke. As soon as we parked in the parking lot, he bolted from the car and threw up in the snow. Mary reached back to hand me something, which I refused, intent on seeing to Michael and intent on keeping my own breakfast down.

"Cover it up," Mary ordered from the front seat of the car. "It's disgusting!"

"No thanks," I replied. "If I get over there, I'll do the same thing."

While Rachel tended to Michael, Mary asked me something else which I couldn't understand. I asked her to repeat herself. She mumbled in the front seat.

"I can't hear you," I explained. "What did you say?"

"Nothing."

What an obnoxious answer, I thought. How passive aggressive can you get? Well, I'm not going to be manipulated. I don't feel well enough to play any stupid games. If she wants to be noncommunicative, then two can sing that tune.

That simple, insignificant event had suddenly, in a way that denied logical explanation, escalated into a major battleground. Pride took over on both sides, and the miserable morning went downhill from there.

During the fifteen-minute gondola ride to the top of the mountain, I kept replaying my wife's insensitive behavior.

How could she be so selfish? And why didn't she listen to me? She never listens to me. I always have to be the one to listen to her. And now she's giving me the silent treatment, pretending nothing is wrong though it must be obvious to everyone on the mountain that very much is wrong.

We exited the gondola and stumbled down the stairs in our clumsy ski boots. They are great for skiing but make for ridiculous walking.

We snapped our skis on and skied over to the Apache Basin, our favorite run. Somehow, Mary and I got separated from the kids, so I took that opportunity to confront her.

"You got angry with me down there, didn't you?"

"I wouldn't say 'angry' exactly. You just didn't listen to me. I tried to give you the Kleenex, and you blew me off. Then you as much as told me to jump in the lake when I suggested you cover up Michael's vomit. And then you pretended not to hear me in the car."

"Pretended not to hear you? I didn't hear you," I protested. "I asked you what you said and you wouldn't tell me. I didn't take the Kleenex because I wanted to get out and see to Michael. I didn't really care about the mess he made. Besides, I didn't want to get near it and follow suit. I told you that. You just didn't listen."

"I'd rather be ignored in private than to be ignored in public," she said.

She hadn't heard anything I had said to her. I could use my counseling skills to get this thing out in the open and deal with it, but suddenly I didn't want to. Why did I always have to be the one to use active listening skills?

Why did I always have to be the rational one? If she'd rather be ignored in private, then I would give her what she wanted!

Without a word, I turned my skis down the steep slope and headed straight to the bottom without traversing. I skied for the chairlift at breakneck speed, thinking, I'll show her. I'll just ski alone. Yeah. I can do that. I'm the daddy in this family. And the best skier. I've had to hold back the whole stupid trip. I deserve a little time to myself.

As I mounted the chairlift alone, Mary skied past below me. "I'll see you later," she yelled. Even from so far away I could hear the hurt and anger in her voice.

I couldn't believe it. How could she just ski off like that? At least I had intended to ski on the same run! Well, she wouldn't manipulate me into staying with the family.

Rachel and the boys were waiting when I got off the lift. "Where's Mary?" she asked.

"She's going to ski alone, for a while. So am I."

"What happened?" Rachel said, her voiced tinged with alarm.

"We had a fight. Well, not really a fight. An almost fight," I lied. "And I need to ski alone for a while. Can you watch the boys?"

"Sure. No problem."

"Good. I'll meet you at 1:30 at the base for lunch." Without another word I pointed my skis downhill and raced to catch the tips. I skied foolishly fast, and my mind raced even faster. I was angry and hurt, and my pride had been wounded. I could not believe that my wife had just run off like that!

Meanwhile, on the other side of the mountain, Mary was having her own adventures fending off some not so subtle attacks of the Evil One. She was angry too. And hurt. How could the man who loved her so deeply treat her with such arrogant insensitivity?

As she got off the chairlift and was adjusting her goggles, an off-duty ski instructor sidled over from out of nowhere and introduced himself. I wasn't there so I can only imagine the interchange and his blinding tan.

"Bonjour, my name is Jean-Claude." The sun radiated off his white teeth, melting the snow in front of him. "I am new in your country. Would you like to ski down the mountain with me? I would be delighted to give you a few, how you say, 'pointers,' if you wish."

Mary has not always enjoyed skiing. It has been a little scary for her, but she has stuck with it because the kids and I like it so much. She has had a number of lessons, and they all helped her improve in some way. Now here was a handsome young man, skilled in the art of instruction, offering to teach her for free at a time when she had been "abandoned" by her moronic husband.

"No thanks," she said, "I'm supposed to meet my husband shortly."

"As you wish, mademoiselle," he replied, dropping to one knee and kissing her hand before dashing madly down the nearest mogul patch.

"Was he trying to put the make on me?" she wondered. "Naw. I'm a minister's wife. I'm just imagining things." Very dangerous words for a lonely, hurt woman skiing alone.

Her run down the mountain was uneventful. Not so her ride up the chairlift. She wasn't alone. This time there were two guys, not ski instructors. Again I can only imagine their approach—not suave and not subtle.

"Hey, chick. Me and Guido was wonderin' if you might wanna, you know, ski down the mountain wit' us. Right, Guido?"

Guido grunts and drools, sniffing Mary's hair at the same time.

"Uh, why, uh, thank you for your kind offer. But I'm supposed to meet my husband soon."

"Yeah? How come any guy in his right mind would let a fox like you out of his sight for a minute?"

"Well…we had a little disagreement about where to ski and…"

"Yuh mean the slob just cut you loose like that? What a jerk!"

"No. No, he's not a jerk. Well, not all the time, anyway."

"Guido, flex for the lady. Lady, you know how hard it is to pop the seams on a ski jacket like that? We'll fix this husband of yours, and then we'll show you a good time, me and Guido."

"That's really interesting the way you can make your neck so large, Mr. Guido. Oh, look. It's time to get off the chairlift. No, I don't think I'll need to ski with you. Hope you fellows have a good time."

"It's okay, lady. If you need us, we'll be around. Come on, Guido. Stop drooling on her skis; you'll freeze 'em solid."

When we met for lunch at the bottom of the mountain, Mary and I had had quite a while to ponder our mutual sins and the temptations that had been placed in our paths.

Both of us had allowed a small incident to get blown way out of proportion. And in our anger, we had allowed the devil a foothold. He took it. Our wounded pride and our anger had opened the possibility for damage to our relationship. For a morning we had given Satan a perch from which to operate.

While my fantasized concept of Mary's encounters is obviously exaggerated, the fact is she was approached twice by men during her absence from me. We have skied separately on many occasions, but this is the only time anyone has approached her. She was particularly vulnerable after our fight, and the enemy knew it. But she wasn't as vulnerable as he thought.

Over lunch we debriefed the family on what had happened. And we apologized all around. I asked to be forgiven for my infantile temper and my irritating way of turning situations around so they seem to be somebody else's fault. Mary apologized for her unwillingness to talk and her tendency towards sarcasm. And we both apologized to the children for messing up their morning.

We love each other, but what we showed on the mountain was not love. We were not patient nor kind. We were proud and we were rude. We sought our own way, and we allowed ourselves to have fuses that were way too short.

We can laugh about it now. But it really wasn't funny. In

our anger we did sin. And we gave the devil a foothold. But, in victory we took it back.

*S*UPERMAN IS DEAD

"The virgin will be with child and will give birth to a son, and they will call him Immanuel"—which means "God with us."

MATTHEW 1:23

SUPERMAN DIED TODAY. The Man of Steel was fifty-four. His passing marks the end of an era: the end of the age of innocence in the twentieth century.

Perhaps by the time this makes its way into your hands, he will have been born again, the way comic book characters sometimes are. But for now he is dead.

When I was a child of five or six, I used to think his power was in the cape. So when Granny safety-pinned bath towels around our necks, I knew I could fly. Carefully and quietly I shinnied up the round-lathed pole holding up her front porch roof on Commerce Street in Denton, Texas. Then, unfurling my towel cape behind me, I would jump from the roof to the not-so-soft earth below.

Sometimes I landed so hard it felt as if my legs were being driven up inside my body. The power definitely wasn't in the cape.

Well, if it wasn't the cape, surely it was the uniform—the blue tights and the red underwear. That's what made him able to leap tall buildings in a single bound, to be more powerful than a locomotive, and to fly faster than a speeding bullet. And look where the bad guys always shot him—in the chest! The bullets just bounced off. Lucky they didn't shoot him in the head. No uniform there. Bad guys can be so stupid.

But it wasn't the uniform.

My next theory was that God, Jesus, Superman, and Santa Claus were somehow connected. You figure. Who knows everything you do, good or bad? Where do good boys and girls go? And what reward do bad children get at Christmas? Who can fly? Who is indestructible and therefore can live forever? And where is Superman's Fortress of Solitude? (Hint: The North Pole.) It seems natural to confuse four such pristine characters.

Then, Virginia notwithstanding, I became disillusioned about Santa Claus. And as I entered my rebellious adolescence, I had serious questions about God and Jesus.

But Superman was the universal constant. He was unbeatable. Superman couldn't feel pain. He never got a crick in his neck. His beard didn't grow. He didn't get tired. He didn't need food or water or even air. Bullets couldn't hurt him. Not even a falling meteor or the nuclear heat of the sun's interior could faze him.

As I was becoming a man, though, as I began to face the

grays of life, I became more and more uncomfortable with the black-and-whiteness of the Man of Steel. He became a victim of his own success. He was so strong no one could best him in a fight, fair or otherwise. He was so powerful that no force in the universe could oppose him and win. He was utterly invincible. And he became ever more boring and ever more removed from my everyday reality, where things were rarely black and white.

The Canadian commentator on the public radio station said the Kryptonian's death was a sign of the times. Superman wasn't a man of the nineties. The Man of Tomorrow was from another age, a bygone era when virtue was hailed and good always won.

Now is the age of gold-dipped yuppies, birth control by death, and cop-killing rappers. More and more our heroes have been wearing tarnished halos. I really think James Bond started it all. He slept with no underwear on, said "damn," gambled, and always ended up in the sack with some exotic babe with a cute, sexy name. Ever since, we have demanded our heroes have clay feet. Wet clay feet.

Then there's Superman. A fifty-four-year-old virgin from another planet. Even his alter ego, Clark Kent, is virtuous—dull, but virtuous. These guys don't even know the meaning of the word *angst*. If Kent can't make the rent for some reason, Superman will squeeze coal into a diamond or find a sunken treasure ship. The only real world problem he/they have is whether someone, like Lois Lane, will discover his/their true identity and blow his/their cover.

So, what does all this have to do with Jesus, eternity, and a secure relationship with God?

The nineties have been hailed as the new spiritual age— the New Age. People are rediscovering their spiritual hunger. Yet, the old spiritual path to God through his son, Jesus, is as worn in many people's minds as Superman. It doesn't seem to fit the New Age. Christianity is filled with uncomfortable absolutes: marriage to one partner for life, chastity before marriage, not cheating on your income tax, having fun without getting plastered, etc. But the New Age is an age of relativity. If Christ is good, he's in everything, and everything is in him, and so anything is okay. No blacks, no whites, just unoffensive grayness. It's a spiritual justification of the sixties' anthem, "If it feels good, do it."

Jesus is a superman. He is divinity. And divinity is intimidating in its perfection.

So we turn to the imperfection of the New Age. We seek inspiration from long dead gods of earth and sea and sun. We embrace the opportunity to redeem our mistakes ourselves through reincarnation. We even seek spirit guides, who have lived before on this earth, to help us find a higher consciousness.

And what of Jesus? For many who are seeking enlightenment, he is viewed as the unreachable star, far away, irrelevant, and disconnected in his perfection. Not because he is, but because that is how the Church has often painted him. So the people, in desperation, try to bring him back within their grasp. They remake him in their own image and in the images of the things dear to them. This is the gospel of the New Age.

Is it any wonder, then, that Superman died? He's so…absolute. It's easy to confuse his "supermanness" with divinity. The combination is daunting. So the publishers have killed him off. And if he returns, which I am sure he will, Superman will be less perfect, more vulnerable. He will be reborn an almost-Superman of the nineties.

And Jesus? Perhaps his "godness" has been emphasized at the expense of his humanness. I know my own experience was almost to throw Christ out as unattainable. I could never be like him. I was too weak, too imperfect. Too human. And he was...superman. That was the popular picture I had gleaned from books, songs, occasional Bible classes, and movies.

Perhaps the problem is with the communicator. Perhaps with the receiver. Regardless, the message has not been received by much of the world.

God chose to become a man for a mysterious reason. It was only by becoming a human being that he could die. And it was only in dying that he could defeat death.[1]

Yet he did become fully human, subject to the same physical and emotional injuries, the same impulses and temptations as you and I. The scripture even claims that he was tempted in every way, just as we are.[2] I read that to mean he has walked the paths I have walked, wrestled with the same passions and temptations with which I wrestle, and experienced the same emotions that have troubled me, and you, and all of humanity.

Jesus is still virginal, still pure. But the thirty-three years he spent as a human being have marked him for eternity. As he stands at the right hand of God, he will always know what it is like to be human. He knows the temptation of not paying his taxes. He knows the seductive tuggings of the senses. He has held back his own raging torrents as the persecutors attacked him for doing good and attributed his deeds to the Enemy. And he experienced the perfidy of Judas, a man he handpicked to follow him and lead others.

Jesus has known both our sorrow and his own. He buried his worldly father and wept over the effect the death of Lazarus had on Mary and Martha. And when he was on the cross, that unique moment in time when all of creation hung between heaven and hell, he felt abandoned and betrayed by the only one who could save him. For an instant that will ever mark the tapestry of time, the Son was separated from the Father. For our sake.

Jesus is perfect, but not in the same way that Superman is. His feet are not made of clay, but they are not of gold, either. Jesus is a true paradox—humanity and divinity in one. He has tasted both the bitterness of grief and the loneliness of perfection.

Jesus is a paradox, and Superman, a parody—a two-dimensional picture of perfection. His Achilles heel was not that he couldn't be tempted, but that there was never any real possibility that he would fall. Jesus, on the other hand, came close, first in the Garden of Gethsemane, and then on the cross. He knew that even though the spirit was willing, the body was weak. "Daddy, you can do anything. Don't make me do this! Don't make me suffer this humiliation and death! Please! But, even so, let's do what you want to do."[3]

And it stung to think that there really was no other way to save mankind than for him to become the very thing his father hated most.

God knew this world couldn't stomach perfection. That's why he sent the Great Reconciler. The one who was both God and man. To live as one of us. To die for all of us. And to be raised to new life which we can all participate in.[4]

Superman died today. I hope we take the hint. We must make people aware of both the Savior's perfection and his possibility of imperfection. People you know, and those you don't know, need to be brought face to face with the biblical Jesus. If they are not, either the world will continue to recreate him in its own image, or there may be another funeral for another superman.

FROM MOMENT TO MOMENT

"Therefore do not worry about tomorrow, for tomorrow will worry about itself. Each day has enough trouble of its own."

MATTHEW 6:34

I CAME INSTANTLY AWAKE, sensing a presence at the side of my bed. Geoffrey, my ten-year-old, stared down at me. I glanced at the clock, and the night glue slowly left my eyes. When I finally focused, the red numerals on the digital clock read 4:55 A.M.

"What's the matter, son?" I asked, leaning on one elbow.

"I can't sleep." His voice was soft.

"How long have you been awake?"

"Two hours."

"That's a long time. What do you think is going on?"

"I don't want to go to school tomorrow."

He had been sick for seven days with a high fever, croup, and congestion. His head had hurt. He had had chills and body aches. He had been miserable, and he had been unable to do any of his makeup work during his absence. Several times over the past few days he had had buoyant periods when his aches and fever subsided. But each time they returned. Today he had been symptom-free since early morning.

"Worried about all the work you have to make up?"

"No. I'm worried about what will happen if I don't feel good."

"How do you feel now?"

"Okay. But what if I don't feel good later?"

"I don't understand," I said.

"What if I go to school and start feeling bad?"

"I don't know. What do you think will happen?"

"I'll go to the school nurse, she'll call Mom or you, and you'll come get me."

"Sounds like a good plan to me."

He just stood there. It was obvious he didn't feel reassured.

It was time for Plan B. "Do you want to lie down here for a minute?"

Without a word he crawled into bed and put his head in the crook of my arm. I began stroking the smooth skin of his body. I thanked God for its coolness. He had been so hot for so long. The coolness was like a rainbow's promise of calmer days after a violent storm.

But beneath the coolness his little body was coiled and tense. I felt his anxiety and wondered what I could do to help him.

His fear was childish, but it was his fear and it was real. For the last two days he had started the day with a low-grade fever that quickly vanished after he got up. For a while he would feel good and read or play. He would watch his mom bake bread and wash the dishes. He'd play a video game.

And then the fever would strike again. It was vicious. It would spike to 102°. Then shoot to 104°. His face would be flushed, and he would be both hot and cold at the same time.

For Geoffrey it was an insidious and frightening experience. He couldn't believe he would ever be well again. Not really well. He expected each bout of wellness to be followed by more fever and pain.

I, as his father, knew better. I knew he would soon be well. He wasn't seriously ill, though he had been very sick. Soon the sickness would go—if not today, then tomorrow.

I continued alternately stroking his arm, his tummy, his leg, his head. I caressed his face. I put as much love and understanding as I could into my hands. And I felt his worry.

"Geoff? Do you know what Jesus said about worrying?"

"No."

"He said not to worry about tomorrow, because there's enough cruddy stuff that happens today. The idea is to enjoy today, and let tomorrow take care of itself."

He didn't say anything, but I could tell he was listening.

"Sometimes it's hard to live one day at a time. Sometimes you have to live one hour at a time. Or one minute at a time. Do you think you might be able to enjoy this minute right now?"

"I think so."

"Go ahead and give it a shot."

I continued stroking him and he lay quietly. After a bit I asked, "Did you enjoy that moment?"

"Yes."

"Good. Now let's see if you can enjoy this moment."

Again I continued to hold him and caress him. I could tell he was enjoying himself. I was, too. Again I asked, "Did you enjoy that moment, Geoff?"

"Yes." He hadn't moved a whisker.

I repeated the process a couple more times with the same result. Then I asked him if he thought he could sleep now.

"I think so," came his quiet voice. This time the fear was completely gone. Only a pleasant tiredness remained.

So I walked him downstairs to his room and tucked him in bed. Again I asked him if he could enjoy this moment. He said yes, so I kissed him good night and went back upstairs.

I was exhilarated! What a smart daddy! What a superb application of Scripture. What a great anecdote this would make someday. I was feeling so smug. After I congratulated myself for about the tenth time, I began to try to go to sleep.

I had to sleep fast, though. I had less than an hour and fifteen minutes before the alarm would go off. I closed my eyes tight. Then tighter. My mind began to churn on all the unfinished business of the week. I wonder if the lady who has been threatening suicide all week will be okay tomorrow? Rats, I forgot to call Glen and tell him about the Divorce Recovery Retreat presentation we are giving at the convention next year. Had I asked Max if he could speak at that meeting? What was that deadline, anyway? Oh, yeah. And what about the couple I had learned were living together. I needed to talk to them this week.

The more I thought, the more I thought. I flipped. I tossed. I fidgeted. Then I got angry with Geoffrey. I was sleeping so well before he woke me up. I'd never get to sleep now. I had too much on my mind.

"Too much on my mind." That's adult-speak for, "I'm worried about tomorrow."

When I realized I was fretting, I argued with myself. "Worrying won't get you anywhere on this stuff; just forget it. Stop thinking about everything and go to sleep." Right.

My mind continued worrying and fussing. I couldn't stop. The more I told myself to shape up, the more I brooded.

Then it hit me. If Jesus' advice was good for my ten-year-old son, it was good for me. I couldn't stop worrying about tomorrow, so I tried not to worry about the next hour. That didn't work either because I might not be able to sleep the next hour.

The moment, Jim. Can you enjoy the moment?

I thought about that. There was no one to hold me and stroke me. Mary was asleep. So I asked God to. And after a minute or so, I asked myself if I had enjoyed that moment.

"Yes," I answered silently.

"I wonder if you can enjoy this moment?" I asked.

I did. And I enjoyed the next one, too, just being in the presence of my Abba, my daddy. And then I enjoyed the next one. And the next. And somewhere along the way I enjoyed the moment so much I drifted into a deep sleep in my daddy's arms.

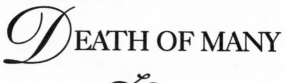EATH OF MANY

Have nothing to do with the fruitless deeds of darkness, but rather expose them. For it is shameful even to mention what the disobedient do in secret.

EPHESIANS 5:11-12

Put on the full armor of God so that you can take your stand against the devil's schemes. For our struggle is not against flesh and blood, but against the rulers, against the authorities, against the powers of this dark world and against the spiritual forces of evil in the heavenly realms. In addition to all this, take up the shield of faith, with which you can extinguish all the flaming arrows of the evil one.

EPHESIANS 6:11-12, 16

I DIDN'T BELIEVE IN DEMONS.

Hey, give me a break. I can remember when the biggest revelation I had was that Christianity was founded on a totally supernatural event—the resurrection. That's fairly fundamental for most Christians, but it took me a while to get there. So it's little wonder that I didn't believe in modern demons. They're not intellectually respectable.

Satan, perhaps, but not demons. I had taught classes about the Father of Lies before. I knew he masquerades as an angel of light in order to pull the wool over our eyes, that he prowls around like a hungry lion bent on our destruction. There is much in the Bible about our adversary. But demons? The most play they get is in the New Testament when Jesus or the apostles are kicking them out of some poor, hapless human. Other than that, the Bible pays relatively little attention to them, so why should I? No sense in majoring in minors.

Besides, I was almost forty-four years old and had been a Christian over half my life. I had never seen a demon, and neither had anyone I knew.

So knowing Dawn has been quite a test for my faith.

Dawn was conceived in a ritual worshiping Lucifer. The union was incestuous, between a parent and grandparent. Intended to be a living sacrifice to the powers of darkness, she has been tortured and brutalized by all the people most of us would look to for safety—mother, father, grandparents, aunts and uncles, doctors, and church people.

It was not long after I met her that Dawn told me about the demons. I was intrigued, of course, but I didn't know whether to believe her at first. I thought she might be hearing schizophrenic voices. And she had already told me she had multiple personalities, so there were lots of explanations for what she experienced other than ugly, little, pointy-headed critters.

But they weren't little. They were huge, according to Dawn. Some were taller than the church building. They were green. Or black. Or blood red. Or purple. Or all four. They had horns and long tongues and sharp teeth and claws.

My first encounter with Dawn's demons was in her motel room. I was accompanied by a woman I'll call Harriet, who had been recommended by a friend. Harriet had a lot of experience with demons, I was told. After introductions we began to pray for Dawn.

Dawn's response was abrupt and intense. She collapsed onto the bed, her body rigid. The catatonia soon gave way to anguished body memories of ritual torture on the altar. Dawn's body writhed in the present while her mind burned decades away, back in the hell of her childhood.

As her body moved, her shirttail came loose, and I saw a tattoo of an insect on her right side, near her waist. As we prayed for her, she grimaced and clutched her side. "It's biting me! Ow! Make it stop biting me! It burns!" She had returned from the past; this was happening now.

We prayed for the biting to stop. She rubbed the tattoo on her side, loosening her shirt more. I could hardly believe what I saw. It was a large, red circle about five inches in diameter with an inverted five-point star inside. It was one of the most incredible things I had ever seen. It looked as if it had been drawn there. Yet it hadn't been. It just...appeared.

Harriet said that Satanists use the inverted star inside a circle of power to represent Mendes, the goat's head of Satan. The demons were letting us know to whom Dawn belonged.

Suddenly, demons were becoming much more real to me. If these were parlor tricks, they were good ones. Real good. I had no explanation for such manifestations. Could the mind have caused such things? Not in my experience nor the experience of anyone I knew. They had come from somewhere, but where, if not from the forces of darkness?

The most chilling manifestation was yet to come. Dawn's face changed. The eyes appeared translucent. They twisted wickedly, and the face was transformed into a mask of evil.

Then she spoke. The voice was not Dawn's but rather a harsh, masculine growl. Yet it was Dawn's, because the sound was made with her vocal chords. It said simply, "She's mine! I'll kill the b___!" Her countenance was exultant and evil.

Harriet prayed against the demon, and I did my best just to hang on. The manifestations subsided, Dawn rested fitfully, and Harriet assured me the demon had left. I wasn't so sure.

The experience was overpowering. I reflected on the events of that night as I began the painful work of reconstructing the pigeonholes in my brain. It was not an easy process.

Sometimes I would try to deny that any of the things I had seen had ever occurred. Other times I tried to chalk them up to Dawn's mental state. Or I would suggest to myself that we had all experienced a mass hallucination. And then I would sweep the table clean and start over. God is good. God is great. He is in charge. Jesus is his son. He came to destroy the work of the devil. That includes demons. Demons existed before. They probably exist now. Maybe.

Meanwhile, Dawn was continuing to have trouble. The demon had not left; it had only pretended to leave. And, in fact, Dawn had thousands of demons. The war was engaged, yet I still wasn't sure what enemy we were fighting.

In preparation for my next meeting with Dawn, I read all the New Testament accounts of demons and their expulsion. They were our model for what happened next.

On the afternoon of my birthday, Mary and I were preparing for some close friends to join us for cake and fellowship. Just before they arrived, Dawn called. She was depressed and wanted to go back home to her parents.

Not a good idea.

I called Mary over, and we began praying over the phone for her. When I said "…in the name of Jesus…," that same demonic voice cut in and cursed me. "We're going to take her tonight! She belongs to us!" The phone was hung up before I could continue.

Dawn was in great danger. If they succeeded in taking her back, her parents would certainly rape her and abuse her in rituals. They were likely even to sacrifice her for her rebelliousness.

I called two of our elders, explained a little of what was going on, and asked if they would help. They were a bit taken aback, but, thank God, they agreed to serve however they could. When my friend arrived for cake, I shanghaied him, left his wife with Mary and the kids, drove over to collect Dawn, and then headed for the church building to meet the elders. A hastily assembled network of people across the city began praying.

Once inside, one of the elders read Psalm 91. Then we began praying. In the middle of the prayer, small red stars within circles appeared on the outsides of both of Dawn's lower legs. The four of us looked at each other and swallowed hard. She collapsed and slid out of her chair to the floor, her left hand clenched in a Satanic gesture—the first and fourth fingers extended and the two middle fingers tucked in. Her T-shirt pulled up as she dropped, and we saw a third star and circle on her stomach.

We attended to her safety and her modesty, and we continued our prayer. Soon her face changed, and trembling I asked, "Who are you?"

There was no response.

"Who are you? What is your name?" I demanded.

The eyes just looked at me, full of contempt and hubris.

Then I remembered to call on the name of Jesus. "In the name of Jesus, I command you to tell me your name."

After a pause, the demon answered, but so softly I couldn't hear.

"What did you say?"

"Griever."

I didn't trust that answer. "Don't lie to me, spirit. What is your name? What is your name? Jesus commands you to tell me your name." My friend was saying the same things. The elders were praying, and observing.

"Death!"

"Don't lie, demon. What is your name?"

"Death of Many!" it said.

"Death of Many is your name?"

"Yes."

"Death of Many, in the name of Jesus, I command you to leave this woman."

The body continued to writhe uncomfortably as it watched me.

"In the name of Jesus, I command you to come out!"

"No."

"You can't resist the power of the name of Jesus," said my friend.

The demon smiled.

I began praying to God, calling on the name of his Son to deliver Dawn. The others did the same. The body writhed and twisted, and still the demon refused to go. We were all praying different things, saying different words, and all having the same effect: the demon continued to resist.

Then one of the elders said, "Jesus is Lord."

Suddenly the demon screamed, "Don't say that!" and Dawn's hands covered her ears.

We caught on quick. We responded with a chorus of chants, "Jesus is Lord!"

Now Dawn's body was on the ground, both hands contracted into horns of Satan. "Those have no power," I said, referring to the hand signs. "You have no power against the name of Jesus. You have no legal claim to this woman. Your invitation was by coercion. She doesn't want you here. This woman claims Jesus as Lord. You cannot stay. There is no place for you here. You must leave. Begone, Death of Many. In the name of Jesus, begone!"

We continued for some time, saying whatever the Holy Spirit provided our mouths and hearts to say.

At some point the spirit began to groan. Then wail. Then the body coughed several times. Then again. And again. Finally, with a long loud cry that increased in intensity until abruptly it stopped, Death of Many was gone. The body completely relaxed, and we praised God for this glorious victory. We wept and prayed and praised the name of Jesus. We were jubilant.

And I had learned a profound lesson.

I had read about demons many times. But I never truly believed they existed. Not today. Not in the scientific twentieth century. And in not believing they existed, I denied the power of Jesus to conquer them.

Now I have come face to face with the forces of darkness, and I have seen them flee before the Name.

My friends and I didn't do everything right. In fact, much of what we did was wrong. We were unfocused and often chaotic, relying more on ourselves than on the power of God. But he knew we were learning. And Jesus never denied us the use of his name.

The experience has given me a new appreciation for the light and caused me to read the Bible with a whole new set of eyes. It has also brought home the wisdom in Jesus' admonition to the disciples to "not rejoice that the spirits submit to you, but rejoice that your names are written in heaven."[1] After meeting those demons, I can more fully rejoice that my name is written in heaven. I never want to share my eternity with them!

I have also learned a profound lesson about those who

worship demons. Dawn's coven claims that Lucifer is stronger than God, stronger than Jesus, that he is the "Most High." They try to make black white and white black. Love becomes hate and hate becomes love. To enhance the charade, many coven members cloak themselves with outward signs of respectability. They are doctors and lawyers and leaders in the community. And they are sometimes leaders in their respective churches. If this is startling, it really shouldn't be. Satan is a liar and the father of lies.[2] Paul warned us that "Satan himself masquerades as an angel of light. It is not surprising, then, if his servants masquerade as servants of righteousness."[3] What better place for evil people to hide than in havens of righteousness?

Today, in your state, in your city, otherwise respectable men and women are meeting in covens and cults in the dark of night to glorify Lucifer. Some are members of churches, some in positions of authority. Others are elected officials. Still others are working men and women. They are involved in murder, torture, and the ritual abuse of their own innocent children.

The tragedy is that Dawn is not a unique case. She represents thousands of men and women with similar backgrounds. And she represents thousands more children who are being victimized by the occult. When the children grow up, sometimes they try to escape. If they fail and are caught, they are often tortured, and sometimes they are killed. Even if they are successful in escaping, they may have tremendous burdens to bear and scars, both physical and psychological, that will last a lifetime.

At this writing, Dawn is more at peace than she has been in her life. But she is at the beginning of a very long road. Its end is not sure. Evil forces are still oppressing her. The cult fears her talking and will likely continue to attack her. And then there are the psychological problems. Multiple personality disorder is neither quick nor simple nor inexpensive to treat.

Dawn needs your prayers. All these men and women, these boys and girls, need your prayers. And the spiritual warriors who are fighting alongside them need your prayers.

Although there are still battles to be waged and captives to be freed, the war was won two thousand years ago.

Thank you, Jesus. You are Lord, indeed.

Maranatha.

WHEN NOTHING WILL FIX IT

Praise be to the God and Father of our Lord Jesus Christ, the Father of compassion and the God of all comfort, who comforts us in all our troubles, so that we can comfort those in any trouble with the comfort we ourselves have received from God.

2 CORINTHIANS 1:3-4

"I NEVER GET ANY GOOD MAIL. Max and John get all the good mail. That's what I get for being a Singles Minister. Even Pat gets good mail. This stuff is worse than 'Occupant' letters!" I was grousing to no one in particular the way we do in the office some days. So Marcelle's words didn't quite connect the first time around.

"It's John Murphy. He has died." She was telling the other secretaries in the front office.

"Huh? Who died?" I asked.

"John Murphy. Medical Center Hospital just called. Lois is on her way there."

"Does she know yet?"

"I don't know. I don't think so."

145

"Has anyone else gone to be with her?" I asked. "Are there any other ministers here right now?"

"Just you and Glen, and he's in a counseling session."

"I better hurry over there. I don't want her to be alone when she hears the news."

Those were brave and noble words, but a wave of panic gripped me as I realized what I had done. What would I say to Lois? What if she fell apart? Should I quote Scripture to her? Which ones? Should I pray? What if the words sounded hollow and trite?

I pondered my dilemma on the way to the hospital. I hated hospitals. And I hated death even more. Hospitals were depressing. And helping people face death seemed so futile. There was no way to fix it. I truly believed that John was in a better place, but I didn't think I could tell Lois that. I didn't want to slide into the pat phrases I had heard so often: "God wanted him home. It's really better this way. You'll get over it. Time heals all wounds." I wanted to help her. But I never felt so inadequate as now.

As I pulled into the hospital parking lot, I wondered if I was the man for the job. I even began to doubt if ministry was really my calling, four years into my new career. Did I really have what it took to be with people at terrible times in their lives? I suddenly wished I had not been in the office that day. Then my face burned with shame, and I thanked God for the opportunity to minister to Lois.

John Murphy was my friend. He was a great lion of a man. Just over six feet tall, he seemed much bigger. His glowing white hair framed a great, majestic head. When we greeted one another as men do, his hand swallowed mine. He was larger than life. Yet his ice-blue eyes were gentle as a fawn's and carried the twinkle of a pixie.

We had served together for a couple of years on the board of a Christian newspaper in South Texas. I had been amazed at John's openness. After all, he was almost twice my age and had been preaching and teaching the gospel for longer than I had been alive. In my immaturity I expected him to be rigid and closed-minded.

I was wrong.

John Murphy had been as open-minded as any man I have known. Lois called him "teachable." Oh, new ideas challenged him, sure enough. He struggled with them. But he struggled! In his early years he had been rigid and right. But he had learned that rightness without grace was anti-Christian, and he had repented of his wayward youth. "How many people have I driven away from Jesus?" he wondered aloud one day. Far fewer than he suspected was my hope. And I knew for a fact that he alone had made more Christians than many of the churches he helped plant.

God had blessed him. And now he had taken him. Yet Lois, the love of his life for forty-six years, was still unaware. It was my job to be there when she learned. To comfort her. To hold her. To be a container for her grief.

"I'm looking for Mrs. Murphy. Her husband was…" I started telling the lady behind the counter in the emergency room.

She looked momentarily panicked as she glanced past me. The lady's discomfort was all the proof I needed that Lois had not been told of John's death. I followed her eyes as she said, "She's down that hall, the first door on the left."

Indeed she was. She wore a stylish sweat suit and a black leather fanny pack around her waist. Her face showed concern but not agitation. Lois' neighbor was with her, along with Virginia Rich, the wife of one of our elders.

I remembered that when my father-in-law had died a couple of years before it was important for people to treat me normally, to act not as if I were a pariah, keeping their eyes downcast and shuffling their feet. "Hello, Lois," I said, looking her straight in the eye. "How's it going?"

"Hi, Jim," she said gripping my outstretched hand with both of hers. "I'm still waiting to see the doctor. I don't know why it's taking them so long."

Her eyes kept flashing past me to the door through which I had entered.

"What happened?"

"John let me off at the store and went to pick up cans. He didn't come back. I waited and waited. I got mad at him for leaving me so long. It's just not like him. I finally walked home. When I got home, the EMS had called and told me to come to the hospital. My neighbor was kind enough to bring me."

"Well, how are you doing?" I asked Lois.

"Oh, I'm doing fine. I'm just worried about John. I want to see him. Why won't they let me see him?" The strain was now evident in her voice. Lois, this beautiful, petite woman with bright, intelligent eyes, is a sensitive, loving, godly woman. I didn't want her to hurt.

"I'm sure they will let you see him soon, Lois. What have they told you?"

"Only that they got a call. Some passerby saw him fall over and called them. When they got there, they found him lying in the grass beside the road." The intake of her breath was sharp and sudden, involuntary, as if she had been struck across the face. "We don't know how long he lay there before they got to him." Her eyes looked at something a long way from that room. Perhaps she was seeing the husband of her youth lying in the weeds, alone. Her brows were pinched with grief and pain.

"Did they say what happened?" I wanted her to keep talking and not get locked up in her pain. There would be time for that later. Now it seemed as if she needed all her resources to deal with the blockbuster to come. I didn't know if it was the right thing to do or not, but I thought it was what I would want someone to do for me.

"They think it was a heart attack. Dr. Martin told him to take it easy. But he wouldn't. He just had to take that trip to Europe. And now this."

"I guess he wants to wear out, not rust out," I chuckled lightly.

"That's John." For a moment a smile graced her face. Then it evaporated. In its place was the dryness of anxiety. "What is taking them so long!" she asked.

At that moment a young man entered. It took a few seconds to realize he was the doctor, he looked so young. He must have been thirty or forty years younger than Lois. I wondered if she was as shocked by his youth as I was.

He introduced himself and then said, "Mrs. Murphy,

I'm sorry to tell you that your husband didn't make it."

Her hands rose to her mouth, unbidden. "What do you mean?" she whispered.

"There was nothing we could do. He was too far gone when the paramedics got there."

Lois's body changed from soft, compliant flesh to brittle wax before my eyes. That's one of the things grief does. It robs you of your flexibility. It's as if your whole system stops and goes into rigid neutral. It's a horrible thing to experience. And a horrible thing to see.

I remembered how important touch had been to me when my father died. Just a touch, a connection with another human being. It made me feel less lost, less adrift. So I touched Lois on the shoulder. I held her arm. I wanted to hug her close, to take away the pain.

Tears welled in my eyes, too. Not for my loss, but for hers. Then I remembered the shortest verse in the Bible and the incredible events that accompanied it.[1]

Mary and Martha are aggrieved at the death of their brother Lazarus, and many Jews have walked the two miles from Jerusalem to Bethany to comfort them. Four days he has been in the tomb and now comes the Master. Both of the sisters accuse him for not saving their brother. "If you had been here, he would still be alive!"

As he goes to the tomb, Jesus is flooded with strong emotion. Indignation fills his heart at the affront Death has given. As the Jews wail aloud, he too is moved. He weeps silently at the cruelty of death and the pain of sin. And his resolve is galvanized.

He reminds Mary that he is the resurrection. Not just in the end times, but now as well. Then he commands the stone to be rolled back from the tomb. And he calls in a strong voice, "Lazarus, come out!"

And Lazarus does. To everyone's amazement, the one who has healed the deaf, caused the blind to see, and raised the newly dead, has now raised a rotting, decaying corpse to life again.[2]

Death will never be the same. Jesus has given a foretaste of what the future holds for the Grim Reaper. No more will he be able to keep his victims bound. No more will he be able to steal life, and joy, and victory from people.

Because Jesus is Lord. He is Lord of the living and he is Lord of the dead.

It is by faith that Lois has been able to clutch victory from such a searing loss. It is by faith that I can see John kneeling before the throne, his face shining with the reflected glory of God. It is by faith, not sight, that we know that John Murphy's spirit will some day be reunited with his body. Yet it won't be his body. It will be a new one, created incorruptible. It won't walk with a limp. It won't have trouble climbing steps. And it won't wheeze and clutch its chest after short bouts of exercise.

So, John, I hope you're getting ready. I hope your spirit is limbering up around the crystal sea, kneeling for painless years before the Ancient of Days, shouting in an inexhaustible voice the glory of the Lamb. Praise him, John, and look forward to the time when you will have that new body—the one that can run all over Heaven and never even breathe hard. Smile, John, and let the twinkle glitter in your eyes. And then laugh. For Lois. And for me.

And for all of us. Laugh at what you have learned from experience and what we know only by faith—Death is not the end.

It is the beginning.

A CONVERSATION
WITH SATAN

He who does what is sinful is of the devil, because the devil has been sinning from the beginning. The reason the Son of God appeared was to destroy the devil's work.

1 JOHN 3:8

CHRISTIAN: I want to thank you for granting this interview.

SATAN: I don't grant "interviews." This is an audience.

CHRISTIAN: Uh, yes, of course.

SATAN: What do you want?

CHRISTIAN: Well, uh, basically I want to ask you about your relationship with God and Jesus.

SATAN: *[growling and throwing up his hands]* Don't say that name!

CHRISTIAN: God or Jesus?

SATAN: THE Name! Don't say it!

CHRISTIAN: Okay, okay. Relax. Let me take a different tack. Throughout history, artists and writers have portrayed you as one who delights in the torment of human beings, as if there were a great struggle between you and God for the souls of men and women.

SATAN: Not true, not true, my dear man.

CHRISTIAN: Please don't call me "your man."

SATAN: Of course. Nothing personal. But to your comment. What a ridiculous bunch of superstitious drivel. Look at me. Do I look like the kind of person who would delight in tormenting innocent people?

CHRISTIAN: Frankly, you don't. The white suit, the nice tan, the carefully styled hair. You look like you work out a lot.

SATAN: *[raising one eyebrow, he studies the fingernails on his extended right hand]* Enough...but I'm no fanatic.

CHRISTIAN: Then where did those ideas about you come from?

SATAN: Certainly not from your Bible. Show me one passage where it says I like to hurt people.

CHRISTIAN: Well, John said you were a murderer from the beginning.[1] And Peter said you were like a roaring lion, prowling around looking for who you may devour.[2]

SATAN: Whom.

CHRISTIAN: Whom?

SATAN: Whom. "Whom he may devour." That's how the

authorized version reads. It seems I know your Bible better than you do.

CHRISTIAN: That may be so, but you haven't answered John's charge that you are a murderer.

SATAN: Surely you don't believe that? Consider the source. John was a...a fisherman. And not a particularly good one at that. What did he know? Sounds like a red herring to me. I've read the book, and it's a hatchet job. All those guys were out to ruin my reputation.

Look, I'm an expert on human nature. I know what people want, and I like to help them get it. But I'm not pushy. I just try to be around when there's an opportunity to help. Sometimes people don't know how to ask for my help. But their actions speak much louder than their words.

CHRISTIAN: What do you mean by that?

SATAN: Hmm. Let me give you an example. Suppose you had been swallowing that claptrap about loving your neighbor as yourself. And then suppose this neighbor—one of your church "family"—does something typically neighborly, like seduce your wife or molest your daughter. Wouldn't you get a little angry? Maybe just a teeny-weeny bit?

Of course you would! You would be enraged! That's when I would step in to help you feel your feelings and help you get it out of your system. It's very unhealthy to stuff such strong emotions, you know. And in your heart of hearts you know that vile person MUST be punished!

CHRISTIAN: That's what you say, but "'it is mine to avenge; I will repay,' says the Lord."[3]

SATAN: *[shrugging]* Once a victim, always a victim. But so what? This sort of thing happens jillions of times every day. Lots of folks welcome my intervention.

CHRISTIAN: They "welcome" your intervention?

SATAN: Sure. Millions of them. Billions. I'm really a very popular guy.

CHRISTIAN: That's incredible! How do you do it? How can you be in so many places at once?

SATAN: Well, of course I can't be everywhere. I'm fast, but not that fast. So I delegate. It's the way to organizational efficiency in the nineties. If I can't be there to help out, I have subordinates as dedicated as I to human welfare. They are strategically placed, continually waiting, watching for any opportunity...to help. And each one is handpicked, personally trained. *[chuckling]* The little devils get a kick out of taking a load off people's backs.

CHRISTIAN: Pardon me, but that seems inconsistent both with the written record and the historical record of mankind. How do you account for the discrepancies?

SATAN: What discrepancies? My enemies will stop at nothing to discredit me. Frankly I can't understand it. Without me, world economies would be in utter chaos. Greed greases the wheels of international commerce.

And I promote mankind's free will. Where would I be without it? I think the key word is "choice." People must always be free to choose for themselves. Without the freedom of choice, men and women are merely slaves to a demanding higher power.

CHRISTIAN: So you would describe yourself as...pro-choice?

SATAN: Absolutely! That describes me to a *T*.

CHRISTIAN: I wonder if we might look at some of those particular discrepancies I was referring to earlier. For instance, the case of the wild man of the Gerasenes. Here is a man who was infested with your...subordinates...demons. They tormented him day and night so the only place he could stay was a graveyard. He cut himself and ran around naked. He was isolated and alone. Weren't your "subordinates" responsible for that man's unhappiness?[4]

SATAN: Of course not! Human beings can be so narrow-minded. Here was a man who chose a lifestyle that fit him but which his peers found unacceptable. My agents simply helped him realize his full potential. It was the smallness of humans which caused him to be isolated and alone.

But let me ask you, what is so good about togetherness? People don't really want to be herded together like rats in a laboratory. They want to be independent. Rugged individualists. I help them do that. My adversary wants to rob them of their uniqueness and turn them into sycophantic cattle. I believe in individual liberty.

CHRISTIAN: It seems appropriate to remind myself that you are described as a "liar and the father of lies."[5]

SATAN: *[eyes narrowing]* I appreciate neither your tone nor your content.

CHRISTIAN: I was only exercising my individual liberty.

SATAN: Enough! You mock me! I will not be mocked by a mere mortal. My purpose here is simple. My adversary has control of the press and many of the pulpits. He is constantly slandering me. I am here to give you puny humans a choice. He thinks he bought and paid for you, but he's wrong! I make that price worthless whenever any of you chooses me over him. It is that simple. [snapping his fingers] All the rest is window dressing.

CHRISTIAN: And how, exactly, do you persuade us to choose you over him?

SATAN: Persuade? No, no, no. You're not listening. I am a simple creature. You make me out like a siren, calling people to be dashed against the rocks. How unkind! I merely allow people—I prefer to call them "folks"—to choose, remember? [narrowing his eyes] And when they choose, I am right there to help them realize their full potential.

CHRISTIAN: Their full potential?

SATAN: All that they can be! I won't allow anything to get in their way. I want to free them from people who tell them what to do. I want to free them from burdensome rules and commitments to small-minded people.

CHRISTIAN: You mean, like relationships?

SATAN: Yes, of course…if they get in the way. What counts is helping them to reach their full human potential, to learn how to rest in their own human nature—self-actualization. Don't you see?

CHRISTIAN: What if they don't reach their full human potential? What if they fail?

SATAN: That's the beauty of it! You can't fail. Everyone who follows my plan gets the same reward.

CHRISTIAN: In for a penny, in for a pound?

SATAN: Of course.

CHRISTIAN: And the reward is…?

SATAN: Why to be with me, of course!

CHRISTIAN: That's what I thought. And it doesn't sound very appealing to me. Oh, the words you use are popular enough, but you are the Devil. And you are bound for the Lake of Fire. What you're peddling sounds like a lot of pride and self-centeredness to me. Forsaking relationships and living for yourself. I think you are purposely deceiving those people.

SATAN: *[eyes narrowing, he glances at Christian]* That is the second time you have called me a liar, human. I believe this audience is just about over. And so is your pathetic life. *[leaning forward, menacingly]*

CHRISTIAN: *[eyes wide, he shrinks back a bit]* You know, I…I belong to Jesus Christ, and…evil cannot touch me.[6]

SATAN: *[flinching backward]* Don't say that!

CHRISTIAN: *[leaning forward]* Jesus is Lord, of Heaven and Earth,…

SATAN: Aaargh! *[clutching his ears, grimacing]*

CHRISTIAN: …and he has guaranteed me a place in the heavenly realms with him[7] where everything is under our feet...including you.[8] So don't threaten me. *[standing]* I've read the book, too, and I know how it ends. The good guys win. And the devils all go to hell.[9] *[He walks out, leaving Satan cringing in his chair.]*

Notes

Chapter 1: A Confession Before We Start
1. Matthew 25:31-46
2. Romans 8:28-39
3. Ephesians 1:18-23
4. Colossians 2:15

Chapter 3: Colder than the Night
1. Habakkuk 1:2

Chapter 4: Answers to Prayer
1. Matthew 7:7-11

Chapter 5: Looking for the Loophole
1. Matthew 5:40-41
2. 1 Corinthians 6:7
3. Matthew 5:38-42, 44-48
4. Leviticus 19:18
5. Proverbs 17:5
6. Proverbs 24:29
7. Proverbs 25:21

Chapter 8: Good Old Ebenezer
1. 1 Samuel 7:12

Chapter 10: Cashew Lust
1. Proverbs 3:12

Chapter 11: The Price of Admission
1. 2 Corinthians 5:20
2. 1 Timothy 3:2

Chapter 12: The Blame Game
1. Romans 6:23
2. 2 Corinthians 12:9-10

Chapter 14: When Good Sam Blows It
1. Mark 12:31
2. Matthew 10:16
3. Proverbs 26:17

Chapter 16: Superman Is Dead
1. Hebrews 2:14-15
2. Hebrews 4:15
3. Mark 14:36
4. Romans 6:4-5

Chapter 18: Death of Many
1. Luke 10:17-20
2. John 8:44
3. 2 Corinthians 11:14-15

Chapter 19: When Nothing Will Fix It
1. John 11:35
2. John 11:1-46

Chapter 20: Epilogue: A Conversation with Satan
1. John 8:44
2. 1 Peter 5:8, King James Version
3. Romans 12:19
4. Mark 5:1-20
5. John 8:44
6. 1 John 5:18
7. Ephesians 2:6
8. Ephesians 1:18-22
9. Revelation 20:10